MW00942184

you mind warming me up a little dinner?" he said with slurred speech. Staggering toward Waverly, he reached out to hug her, and Waverly stepped back.

"You warm up your own dinner if you can manage to do so without burning down the house. I'll bring some blankets out for you so you can make yourself comfortable on the sofa." Nevin staggered behind Waverly, fighting hard to keep his balance.

"On the sofa?" Nevin stopped and stared at Waverly, his body slowly moving back and forth. He was so drunk he almost tilted backward but was somehow able to keep from doing so. "What do you mean on the sofa? This is my house and I am sleeping in my room tonight, with you, where I belong."

Waverly walked up to stand in front of Nevin. "So help me God, Nevin! If you try to come anywhere near our room tonight, I will pack my children up and walk out the door, never to return! You have got two months! Do you hear me? Two months," Waverly said while holding up two fingers. "Just two months to get your drinking under control. If you don't, my children and I are leaving."

"Well, I'll tell you this one thing, Waverly, you didn't bring *our* children into this world by wishing it so. You may have brought *your* children into the world that way, how, I'll never know. Maybe you know something I don't, heaven forbid!" Nevin burst into uncontrollable laughter. He stopped to catch his breath. "Now you just think about that, Miss Holier-Than-Thou," he said while leaning so far forward Waverly was sure he was going to fall on his face. "What has gotten…" Nevin tried to think of what he was supposed to say next, but he was so drunk he couldn't finish the sentence.

"As I said, Nevin, you've got two months to get control of your drinking before I pack myself and my children up and leave you! I will not let you destroy my children, Nevin, not mentally, physically, or any other way possible!" Waverly paused and fought to bring her temper under control and lower her voice. She lowered her voice and said calmly, "You are Bray's father, not he yours! Yet my son is killing himself trying to take care of his father, worrying himself sick day and night that one day, *one day*, Nevin, he is going to walk in this house only to learn that you never will again because you've killed yourself while driving under the influence!"

Waverly stormed out of the room and returned with a blanket and pillow. She tossed it on the sofa and started to walk back out of the room. "I am your husband, Waverly. How dare you try and keep me out of our bedroom!"

"*No*, you are not my husband. I don't know who you are, but you are certainly not the man I married. Good night, Nevin."

*****

Cree looked down at the slip of information Jessica had given her with her contact information on it. She had about an hour before her next scheduled surgery. It was a beautiful day, temperature in the mid-seventies. The leaves on the trees that towered over her head and on the trees surrounding her moved slightly in reaction to the caress of a gentle breeze.

She took a sip of her iced tea and looked around the grounds of the hospital. *What a beautifully kept sitting area,* she thought. The area was situated in the back of the hospital and led to the emergency room entrance. Cree often visited the area to clear her head, to relieve some of her stress in between surgeries. She couldn't believe it. "Jess? Jess has cancer?" She swore out loud and walked over to sit on a bench. She stuck the slip of paper in the pocket of her medical jacket and then slowly took it back out again.

"I can't do this, I can't allow myself to get involved with Jess in any way. I don't know if I can trust her. If I can trust that she won't just go off on me again for the least little reason," Cree said to herself. Still, she found herself pulling out her cell phone and dialing Jessica's cell number that was written so neatly on the slip of paper alongside Jessica's address.

"Hello, this is Jessica, I'm not available right now. If you don't leave a message, you never should've bothered to call," was the greeting Cree received from her answering machine. Jessica's voice was so clear and understandable, the result of private schools and nothing but the best education from first grade through college.

Cree smiled to herself. "All that expensive education and the woman has never had to work a day in her life." *Oh, Jessica, how fortunate you are.* As Cree thought about Jessica being fortunate, she then remembered she was battling cancer. She looked down at the ground and said, "Well, I guess there will always be *something* in the life of all."

Cree put her cell phone back in her pocket. Ten minutes later, it rang. "Hello."

"Cree? Hey! You tried to call me? Now I know who this number belongs to and trust, I will be using it! I am so glad to hear from you! Come over, are you free? I will make us some lunch. I remember what you like! Shrimp salad, light on the dressing and heavy on the veggies! Did I get it right?" Cree paused. "Cree, are you there?"

"Jess?"

"What? Come on over, silly! Your salad will be waiting." Cree hung up since Jessica had already done so. Shaking her head slowly and sighing heavily, Cree said softly to herself, "How does she manage to do this? How does she manage to talk me into doing just what she wants?" Jessica's house was only six minutes away. If she left now, she reasoned, she could make it in time to have the salad and head back in time to perform her scheduled surgery.

Cree pulled up in front of Jessica's house after driving up to and around her circular driveway. She stopped, put her car in park, and stared up at what looked like a castle. The lawn was immaculate with flowers and beautiful shrubbery everywhere. Walking up to a huge black door, she paused, took out her lipstick, and smeared a little on her lips before ringing the doorbell. She stood there waiting and asking herself, "Cree, what are you doing here? You need to turn around and get back in your car right now, right now!"

Jessica swung open the door suddenly. "Hey! Get in here!"

"Jess, I can't stay long. I have surgery scheduled. I just..."

"No worries, your salad is ready. I have a tall glass of lemonade ready for you too. It will take you all of fifteen minutes to eat it and you can be on your way. Besides, you must eat lunch, right?"

"This room is…"

"Huge!" Jessica said. "Yep, it is, but Dad insisted he buy this house for me!"

"It's beautiful!"

"Come on, let's go to the kitchen. It's an eat-in." Cree followed Jessica to the kitchen and noticed a long winding wrought iron staircase leading to another level of the house. Cree guessed there must be several levels to the house. It was massive!

The wall behind the staircase boasted several family pictures. Jessica's mom stared at her from the surrounding family photos. Her framed portrait stood out from the rest of the pictures in height and width. Jessica's mom was nothing less than stunning. Jessica got her amazing looks and features honestly, Cree concluded.

Cree and Jessica sat down at a kitchen table that could easily seat eight people comfortably. After clearing her throat, Cree said, "Jess, the salad looks wonderful and I really appreciate it, but this is not a social call." Jessica sat a basket of French bread on the table and looked at Cree.

"*No!* Don't, Cree! Please just don't! I do not want to talk about the cancer! I'm sick of it!" Jessica realized what she'd just said and smiled. "No pun intended," Jessica said and licked her lips. "Cree, it is what it is! I can't change things, but I don't have to limit my enjoyment of life while I still have it. I am going to live every single day as though it was my last because…" Jessica looked down at the floor before saying, "it just might be. So please eat your salad and let's catch up." Cree looked at Jessica and then slowly picked up a forkful of shrimp salad and ate it.

Jessica picked up her glass of lemonade and drank from it slowly. "So what are you doing this evening? There is a new movie out, or we could go shopping? Why don't you let me treat you to a new wardrobe! It would be fun, just like old times! You…me, shopping our hearts out and running up Dad's credit card bill," Jessica said and then burst into laughter.

Cree ignored her and said while staring straight at her, "I want to examine you, Jess."

"No!"

"Jess, please?"

"Cree! I said no! I've seen a doctor, endured test after test, MRIs, I'm tired. I want to live my life, Cree, free of all that! I don't want to do it anymore! Please!" Cree knew she was asking for a serious argument but so what! She'd rather argue with Jessica now and hopefully be able to share another lunch with her later someday.

"Jess!"

"All right, that's it, Cree! I want you to leave right now! I told you I didn't want to discuss it!"

"Put me out!"

"What did you just say?" Jessica stared at her in disbelief. "Did you just tell me to put you out?"

"My office, tomorrow morning, Jess, be there and come prepared to be examined! Where is it?"

"Where is what?"

"This is not a joke, Jess. Where is the cancer?" Jessica didn't say anything for a minute.

"It's breast cancer. I've already told you I've seen a doctor and I have accepted his diagnosis. I must face reality, Cree!"

"You said you've seen *a doctor*. Have you considered getting a second opinion?" Unbearable silence hung in the air between them. "Have you?" Jessica turned away and let out a heavy sigh but said nothing. "I didn't think so," Cree said just above a whisper. Cree looked at Jessica sadly before saying, "So are you just going to give up! Is that it! Is that what you've decided to do Jess!? I never figured you to be a quitter Jess, not you!"

"Cree, this is real life, *cancer*! You can't beat this!"

"Maybe not, but I'm sure going to try. My office, tomorrow…eleven o'clock. I'm on the eighth floor. I will leave word with security to expect you and to allow you up. I've got to go. Thank you for the salad. It was good, what I got to taste of it!"

*****

Waverly stood outside Cree's office, hoping to catch her on the way out headed for home. She knew she had a scheduled surgery earlier, and it wasn't an easy one. She wanted to give her time to gather herself before heading home.

The door to Cree's office opened, and she walked out. She looked tired and anxious. "Rough one?"

"*Rough* isn't the word for it. I thought that the more surgeries I performed, the easier it would get physically and emotionally, but it doesn't. What's going on? You need a ride home?" Waverly didn't answer; she walked over and sat down on the bench outside Cree's office and looked up at the ceiling, searching for words to explain how she was feeling, but honestly there were no words.

"Nevin came home drunk again last night." Cree walked over and flopped down beside her. She stretched out her legs and crossed them at the ankle and then rubbed the back of her neck.

"Waverly, you've got to do something about this. Maybe it's time you gave Nevin an ultimatum?"

"I did. I told him he had two months to pull it together with his drinking, or I was going to pack up the kids and leave."

"Yeah? But did you say it like you meant it? Nevin needs to understand that there are consequences for his actions."

"Oh, I meant it! I've had it, Cree! I can't take much more of this!"

"Come on, let me take you home," Cree said softly.

"Thanks, but I drove today. I just wanted to talk for a second. Thanks for listening."

"Sure, anytime!" Cree's thoughts turned to Jessica. "Jess has cancer." Waverly looked at Cree in shock.

"What!"

"It's killing me, I can't let her die, Waverly, I just can't! I'm going to fight it with all I've got! She is not the same Jess I grew up with. She's scared. She tries to hide it, but it's there. I can see it."

"I'm so sorry, Cree."

"Yeah…me too."

*****

MY FATHER, MY SON

Jessica arrived at Cree's office five minutes early. She knocked gently on her door and then slowly turned the handle to open it. Walking slowly into the room and closing the door behind her, Jessica stood and looked around the room, taking in its small size with large frames of Cree's medical degrees. She smiled and said to herself, "Cree is the head of surgery here, yet such a tiny office. Neat but tiny. I wonder where she is?" Noticing the picture of Dylan on the desk, Jessica walked toward it, her eyes fixed on the cute Dylan with long black hair curled to frame her face and large brown eyes. Cree was posed behind her daughter with her arms holding her from the back and around her shoulders with a big smile.

"Hi, Dylan, hi! It's Auntie Jess, I've missed you. But that's okay, we are going to make up for all the lost time. You are a teenager now, so I am going to make sure you have everything a teenager needs from the best phone to the most fashionable clothing. That you can be sure of."

"The phone she has is fine and her clothes may not boast designer labels, but they are clean, and any teenager would be proud to wear them."

Jessica turned around to face Cree with a smile. "Hey, I didn't hear you come in. Dylan, she is all grown up now. She looks just like you, Cree."

"You think so," Cree said while turning up her nose. "I think she is much cuter than I was when I was her age, plus I've never had hair like that a day in my life. At least, that's something I can thank her dad for."

"Still carrying a torch?"

"Come on, Jess, you know me better than that. The torch died the day he left me alone to raise Dylan on my own."

"Hey, well, it looks like you did just fine on your own. But no worries, girl, I'm here now and you know I've got your back when it comes to Dylan."

"Thanks, Jess, you always did spoil her. Heaven only knows what I'm going to be up against now, trying to keep you from doing so." They both laughed.

Cree's smile faded as she looked at Jessica with concern. "When was the last time you had a mammogram?"

"I don't remember. I mean, what is the point of having them now? The dreaded C word has taken up residency in one of my lovelies," Jessica said as she pointed to her breasts with a smile. Jessica's response annoyed Cree.

"I'm not smiling, Jess. It doesn't matter, I've ordered you one for today. When you leave here, you need to go downstairs to the second floor and see Gloria. You can't miss her. Her desk is right there as you get off the elevator. Just walk up to the desk and give her your name and she will take it from there. They are waiting on you. But first, I'd like to give you a thorough examination."

"Cree, please don't make me do this."

"I'm not making you do anything, Jess. You are a grown woman, free to walk out of here anytime you'd like. But I think you know there isn't a doctor anywhere on this earth that's going to fight for your life as hard as I am, so it's to your advantage to stay here." Cree walked over and opened the doors to the adjoining examining room and said, "Let's do this." Jessica hesitated and then threw her purse down in one of the small guest chairs and walked in the room.

"Everything has to come off, including the gorgeous earrings you're wearing. As a matter of fact, you can leave those with me," Cree said with a smile.

"Don't count on it, not after putting me through this." Jessica rolled her eyes at Cree and started to undress.

"I left an examining gown for you. Please put that on when you're done undressing. I will be back in about ten minutes." Cree pulled the doors to the examining room together, walked to her desk, and sat down. She put her head in her hands and said, "Dear God, please help me survive this because I know Jessica is going to fight me every step of the way on whatever treatment I suggest."

*****

"Come on, man! Get in the game, Bray!" Sweat poured from every team member on the floor, both that of DeMassi High and the opposing team members. Jermaine ran up behind Bray and shouted to him a second time, "Bray! Get in the game, man! Where are you?"

There were two minutes left in the game, and DeMassi High was one point short of winning the championship game! Bray fought off an opposing team member so he could take the three-point shot that would win DeMassi the game! Bray took the shot, but the ball hit the rim and bounced off! Bray couldn't believe it! He swore under his breath and ran down the court like a maniac, fighting for another chance to get the ball and take a three-point shot!

There was now a second left in the game! Bray stole the ball from the opposing team, attempted another three-point shot, and missed again! Jermaine rushed up behind

Bray and grabbed the ball before the opposing team member's hands could touch it and dunked the ball in the basket, winning the game for DeMassi! The crowd went wild, and Bray hung his head because he knew all too well why he missed both shots. His mind was on his dad and his coming home too drunk to stand. Instead of being able to fully concentrate on the shots that would win his team the championship, his mind kept reverting to visions of his dad on his hands and knees on the floor and so drunk he couldn't even pick himself up.

Bray and Jermaine sat in Jermaine's jeep in front of the Berman home. "Bray, look, don't sweat it! We won the game, man, and that's all that matters." Bray turned and stared out the window.

"I carry the nickname Hoop because I've never, *never* missed a three-pointer, and tonight I missed two back-to-back. Do you know how that makes me feel, man?"

"You gave it your all, you played your heart out tonight! I know what's up, Bray. It's your dad! I know it is! Bray, I'm telling you, you've got to release it, just let it go! Don't let him destroy you, destroy your future!"

"Jermaine, we are talking about my father, man, my father! What am I supposed to do? Just look the other way, pretend he is not an alcoholic? Pretend that he may—*just may*—make it home every day, knowing that he could kill himself any day now, or worse, someone else, because of his driving while being too drunk to even see straight! Look, I got to go! Thanks for the ride!" Bray opened the door to the jeep and started to get out.

"Bray, hold on, man. Just hold on a minute."

"What, J?"

"Bray, you know my dad is a cop. Maybe I could get him to talk to your dad..."

"And what would he say to him? 'You know, Nevin, you really need to try and get some help before it's too late because if you kill somebody, I'm going to have to arrest you!'" Jermaine looked at Bray, he didn't know how to respond to what he'd just said.

"Thanks, J, but no thanks. Later, man!" Bray got out and ran up to his house, unlocked the door, and then turned and gave Jermaine a slight wave. He wanted him to know he wasn't upset with him. Jermaine smiled sadly and gave him a slight wave back.

When Bray opened the door to his house, Waverly, Ellis, and Noel shouted "Surprise!" Bray stood there for a minute, trying to figure out what was going on.

"What's all this?"

"It's your celebratory surprise, and there is cake in the kitchen. Mom also made your favorite meal...hot dogs and cheese fries. She went a little heavy on the cheese too," Noel said with a big smile on her face. They all laughed except Bray. "Bray, come on, baby, in my heart, I feel you played the best game ever tonight! I know what you were up against on that floor tonight, where your thoughts were, and what made you miss those shots. I couldn't have been prouder of you because you kept fighting hard out there despite all you were going through mentally and emotionally tonight. Now pick your head up and let's go celebrate our victory tonight."

Bray smiled at his mother and hugged her. "Thanks, Mom."

A few seconds later, Noel opened the door to let Jermaine in. Jermaine walked in with a sheepish grin on his face. Bray looked at him, saying, "I think you somehow had something to do with this, J." Jermaine laughed. "Had something to do with it? I suggested it! Come on, man, let's go grab a dog and some of those cheese fries… Your mom makes the best and I'm hungry!" They all laughed this time and walked to the kitchen to celebrate.

*****

Waverly walked out onto the deck with a cup of ice-cold lemonade in her hands. She took out her cell phone and checked for any calls from the hospital, which was the norm for her every evening. After having a seat in one of the big wicker winged-backed chairs, she looked around at the large colorful pots of flowers and ferns that decorated the deck. Her thoughts drifted to Cree, and she thought about calling her to come over and join her on the deck.

A beautiful sunset made her turn her attention from the flowers to the sky. She sat and stared at the beautiful golden orange sky with a hint of blues and grays. The sound of crickets, or summer bugs as she liked to refer to them, broke the silence of the evening but also added to the relaxed feeling that came over her. Her cell phone rang, and she looked down at it; it was as if Cree had read her mind and called her first.

"Hey! I was just about to call you!"

"What are you up to?"

"I am just sitting here on the deck with a glass of lemonade and enjoying the evening. What about you?" Cree didn't say anything, causing an unbearable silence, and Waverly instantly knew something was wrong.

"Cree? What? What is it? What's going on? Tell me! Is Dylan okay?"

"I got the results of Jessica's mammogram back today." Waverly was scared to ask, but she would go insane if she didn't know what the result was.

"And…" Silence again.

"She has stage two breast cancer, Waverly."

Neither of them said anything right away; they both just sat there and held the phone to their ear for a minute. "I'm a doctor, a surgeon. I've seen it all, dealt with it all! So why is this so hard for me to accept, to deal with?" Cree said as she started to cry.

"I'm coming over. I'll be there in a few minutes, a few minutes." Waverly ended the call and slowly laid her phone down. She then walked to the banister of the deck and tossed her lemonade out.

When Waverly arrived at Cree's house, she walked slowly to her door. Once she was standing in front of it, she paused before knocking and pressed her hand to her stomach to calm herself, get control of her emotions. When she felt she was okay, she knocked on the door. Cree opened the door slowly. Waverly looked at Cree, and they both broke down and cried.

Chapter 9

"Can you believe it, in less than two weeks, we graduate from high school? I can't wait!"

"Dylan, bring it down a notch. Your mom is upstairs sleeping, remember?"

"Sorry, I'm just so excited I can hardly stand it, Noi!"

"Where is everyone? It's Monday night. Our chat session was supposed to start ten minutes ago." Dylan and Noi looked toward the door as Jermaine rushed in and took a seat.

"Traffic! I thought I was going to have to park my jeep, get out, and jog here it was so bad." Noel looked at Jermaine and said to herself, *God, that boy is fine!* "Bray and Ellis are right behind me," Jermaine said and leaned his head against the back of the sofa to relax and catch his breath.

TJ walked in shortly after Bray and Ellis, carrying two large bags of pretzels. Noel looked at her, surprised! "I thought you texted me you were picking up corn chips?"

"What? They had sold out of corn chips, and I was too tired and too late to go running all over town looking for corn chips, Noi! Besides, we have pizza and salad tonight, we should be fine!"

"Well, isn't this session getting off to a terrific start," Dylan said sarcastically. Noel looked at Dylan.

"Do you have the cupcakes?"

"Yep, they are in the kitchen. Do you want me to get them now, Noi?"

"Nope, I just need to know we, at least, have those."

"Okay, guys, we are already late. This Monday's chat session should have started already. So everybody grab a plate, plop some food on it, and let's go. The floor is open, anybody care to start?" Noel said while looking around the room. Nobody said anything; they were too busy eating. "Okay then, I'll start. I think Dylan has something to say to TJ…in front of the group?"

"Noi, what is going on? I've already sent a group text to TJ apologizing to her for what I did last session! Can't you just let it go already?"

"No…I can't, I won't! You said what you had to say to TJ in front of everyone last session, Dylan. She deserves an apology in front of everyone…don't you think?" Dylan stared at Noel. The room became very quiet. "Okay then, let's take a vote." Noel took a sip of her Sprite and looked around the room before saying, "Everyone who thinks Dylan should apologize to TJ in front of the group for what she said to TJ last session, please raise your hand."

Everyone raised their hand except TJ and Dylan. "Noi, she did apologize to me already, it's cool. Let's just move on to something else, okay?" Dylan jumped up.

"You know what, Noi is right. I do owe TJ an apology in front of the group."

Dylan walked swiftly to the front of the room, stood beside Noel's chair, and turned her attention to TJ. "Let the record show that I, Dylan Hayes, *sincerely* apologize to TJ for putting her on the spot last chat session… I'm sorry, TJ." Dylan then walked back to her seat and sat down.

"Okay, now that we have that out of the way, anybody else?" Dylan raised her hand. Noel was terrified of what might come out of Dylan's mouth after having been made to apologize to TJ. She stared at Dylan for a second. "Dylan…you have the floor."

"I'm excited about graduation. It's right around the corner for me, Bray, and Jermaine. But I'm sad that the three of us will be going off to college and leaving Noi, TJ, and Ellis. I mean, I can't believe it!"

Jermaine looked at Dylan and said, "Neither can I."

"Hey, even more reason for us to cherish the time we all have left together. "Let's throw a barbecue next weekend. We can have it at my house!"

"Are you sure, Noi?"

"Of course, just leave it all up to me, Dylan. It will be great!"

"Awesome! But there is one other thing I'd like to discuss with the group." Dylan looked down at the floor and then looked up at everyone. "My mother's…my mother's best friend from high school, I call her Aunt Jess, she has… she has cancer. I can't believe it and I'm scared. She looks so beautiful, strong, and healthy-looking." TJ raised her hand, and Noel called on her.

"You know, I've heard that a person can be really sick yet not look like they are sick." Everyone started throwing in their comments, adding to what TJ said without raising their hand, and the session was getting out of control.

"Guys, wait, hold on a minute, one at a time, please!"

"Sorry, Noi, I'd like to say something."

"Sure, Ellis, you have the floor." Ellis turned to Dylan.

"Dylan, I'm really sorry to hear about your mom's friend. It sounds like you three were really close. I seriously hope she will pull through it. Cancer, that's scary. Your mom is an excellent doctor. Her friend is very fortunate to have her in her corner."

"Thank you so much, Ellis. I really appreciate you saying that."

"We are all here for you, Dylan. Anytime you need to talk, take a walk, cry, whatever! You know we've got you, right? We are all here for you no matter what time of the day or night. Right, guys, we all understand this, right?" Noel said. Everyone chimed in with their agreement to being there for Dylan whenever she needed them.

"Hey, guys, I have some news. Sorry I forgot to raise my hand."

"Go ahead, Bray, what's up?"

"Thanks, Noi. I got it! Found out today! I got a full-paid scholarship to the college of my choice!"

"What!" Dylan said and ran over to Bray. Everyone else started cheering and giving each other a high-five.

"Bray, that is so awesome! I am so proud of you, man! I knew it!"

"Thanks, Jermaine!"

*****

Jessica opened her door to find Cree standing there with a folder in her hands. She didn't say anything, just turned and walked over to the sofa and sat down. Cree walked in and stood in front of her, not even bothering to close the door behind her. Cree looked at the folder in her hand and then pointed it at Jessica. "How long, Jess? How long have you known about the cancer?" Jessica looked up at her.

"I told you to leave it alone, Cree, but no, you had to know more, examine me, have another mammogram done."

"I said, how long have you known?" Cree shouted at her.

Jessica ignored her and looked down at the floor. "You've known for a while, haven't you? Why, Jess? Why did you wait? You're at stage two cancer now. The only way this could have happened is that you didn't know it was there or…or heaven forbid, you knew and didn't seek treatment!"

"I've already told you that Dad and I spent money, a lot of money, trying to get me the help I needed. We tried, Cree!"

"A mastectomy, Jess, did you ever consider that? I can't believe I'm standing here in front of you, practically begging you to do what you know you should have done a long time ago. Get the treatment you needed a long time ago, and you are acting as if we are talking about a migraine, Jessica! This is cancer, it can and will kill you if it goes untreated."

"Okay, now you hear this, Cree! You mentioned a mastectomy! Yes, I was told that it was necessary and radiation treatments. I've had radiation treatments. A mastectomy? I would rather…rather *die* than go through life maimed and bald! I want to get married someday, Cree. What man is going to want a sliced-up and bald woman? Like I said, I would rather die than go through life that way."

Cree walked over and sat down beside Jessica. "All right, Jessica, I listened to you, and now you hear this. Your breast cancer has progressed to stage two. If it is allowed to progress to stage three, it will spread beyond your breast and into nearby lymph nodes and muscles. Stage four, referred to as advanced breast cancer or metastatic breast cancer, will have spread to other parts of your body. Breast cancer will metastasize in any part of your body, but the most common areas are your bones, lungs, liver, or…brain."

Cree paused and stared at Jessica to see if what she'd just said was having any effect on her. Jessica looked down at the floor again but said nothing. Cree looked at Jessica and said just above a whisper, "Jess, there is more than one growth. You do know this, right?"

"Of course I do! I have been through all of this, Cree, told everything, radiation treatments, all of it!"

Cree held her hand up and shook her head in frustration; she was getting angry. "Stop, just stop! This is me, Jess! I know you, so you can't talk your way out of this! Excuses! You're trying to hand me a bunch of freaking weak excuses! Well, you should know me well enough by now to realize that excuses don't work with me. Jess, if what I just said to you isn't registering, maybe this will. If you don't get the treatment you need, and I mean fast, you won't have to worry about a man wanting to take you for his wife maimed, bald, or any other way because you *will* be dead! You know my number, call me when you grow up and you're ready to deal with this. I just hope and pray for your sake it won't be too late." Cree got up and stormed out the door, slamming it behind her.

By the time Cree returned to her office and sat down after leaving Jessica's house, she was so upset she was shaking. Her cell phone rang; Jessica was calling. Cree answered the call with hesitancy and nervousness. "Jess?"

"I'll have the mastectomy and the radiation treatments." Cree swallowed back tears.

"Thank you, Jess, thank you so much."

"Why are you thanking me? I should be thanking you, I'm the one with cancer."

"I don't know, I don't care. I'm just glad you've agreed to fight it!"

*****

A week had passed since Jessica's mastectomy, and she was doing great! She only needed partial radiation treatments. She experienced some hair loss, but she had so much hair you couldn't tell. Cree and Waverly sat with her in her kitchen eating triple fudge chocolate cake and ice cream. They laughed, joked, and planned to see a play over the weekend.

Jessica looked at Waverly. "I'm glad Cree gave me the opportunity to apologize to you that night after you left Dad's restaurant and sat in the car. I could have lost a very good friend, you Waverly! I am so happy to have both of you in my life and I can't wait to start nurturing our friendship, that thanks to Cree and her persistence I think I'm going to have a long time to do." They all smiled and finished off their cake and ice cream.

Chapter 10

"Dylan, it's Saturday and you're talking like you have somewhere to be in the next five minutes. Slow down! I am glad we are having the Monday Night Chat Session Cookout next Saturday instead of this Saturday so we can shop for the prom."

"Listen, Berman, I don't want to be getting to the mall at, like, six this afternoon only to find that the shoes I picked out to wear with my prom dress have been picked out and bought by someone else! I knew I should have just bought those shoes when I first saw them! But no, I had to listen to you."

"Dylan, those shoes were, like, two hundred bucks, are you serious? For one night?" Dylan sighed heavily.

"Bray, I can see right now that when we get married, money is going to be an issue and you know why? Because you're cheap!"

"Not cheap, frugal! There is a difference. I've got to hit the shower. I'll be at your house at twelve. I'll drive, Mom is letting me take her car, which means more room for more bags, and I like the color red. She is taking my car," Bray said.

"Okay, see you at twelve."

Bray ended the call with Dylan and stared down at his cell phone while thinking, *Dylan is going to drive me crazy before I even turn twenty years old.* Thinking back over the conversation he and Dylan had just finished, Bray's mind lingered on the thought of him and Dylan getting married, a decision they made about a year after they started seeing each other. They'd discussed it and realized that even though they were very young, neither of them could see spending their life with anyone but each other. "I can't believe I let her talk me into our one day getting married." Bray smiled to himself as he remembered the conversation. "Really, Bray, truth be told, you were the one who talked Dylan into wanting to marry you one day," Bray said to himself.

Bray sniffed; he could smell them, the scent lighting up the entire house. The smell of his mother's blueberry pancakes on a Saturday morning. He jumped up off his bed, rushed to the bathroom to wash his face and hands, and then threw on a sweatshirt over his pajama bottoms.

"Pancakes! Pancakes! Mom's blueberry pancakes," Bray yelled as he ran down the hall and banged on the door of Noel and Ellis. "Be late and they will be gone!" Noel sprang up and threw on a pair of jeans and a shirt! Ellis, already half dressed, picked up a hoody from his floor and threw it on over his shorts.

Noel and Ellis came running out of their room at the same time and almost knocked each other down trying to get to the bathroom before the other one to wash up! They made it to the bathroom at the same time after pushing and shoving each other along the way in an effort to be the first to make it to the bathroom door.

They stood in front of the bathroom door, staring each other down. "No way, Ellis, no freaking way! I made it to this door first and I'm going in first!"

"Oh yeah! I'd like to see you try! I got here first, Noi, and you know it, so step aside!"

"Mom!" Noel yelled downstairs to her mother! Waverly looked up as she set a plate of blueberry pancakes in front of Bray.

"Those two! Ellis, let your sister use the bathroom first. Ladies first, son," Waverly yelled up to them. "Oh my goodness, now they've got me yelling! You would think that by now your brother would know to let your sister use the bathroom first," Waverly said while shaking her head. Ellis pushed Noel playfully and then stood back and let her go in the bathroom first.

Waverly sat down at the table opposite Bray and looked at her son, pride causing her chest to rise. Bray didn't notice his mother looking at him; he was too busy downing his pancakes and orange juice. Waverly smiled and cleared her throat to get his attention.

"So, my future author, scholarship paid in full to the college of your choice. I am so proud of you, baby. I kind of suspected it, but now that it's really happened, I don't know what to say." Bray finished off his last bite of pancake, followed by a sip of his orange juice.

"Thanks, Mom. I can hardly believe it myself. When Coach and Principle Warren said they needed to see me, I thought I was in trouble."

"You, in trouble? Never! Well, I'm waiting! What college have you decided on?"

"Mom, you know all my life practically ever since I was about ten years old. All I've ever talked about was becoming a writer, it's my passion! I've researched a couple of colleges and I've narrowed it down to one, Northwestern University!" Waverly set her glass of orange juice down and smiled.

"Bray, that is an excellent choice! I'm so happy for you!"

"What is an excellent choice," Noel asked as she sat down at the table and started filling her plate with pancakes.

"Your brother has decided to go to Northwestern University!"

"You go, Bray, my brother the writer! You are going to make an excellent writer. I have an idea for your first book," Noel said excitedly!

"Oh really, let's hear it!"

"I want you to write about my life, Bray. It will be easy! I mean, how could it not be? My life is so interesting, you know!" Ellis, who had walked in and sat down shortly after Noel, burst out laughing.

"Your life, interesting? Sure, if you call mothering people to death interesting." Noel rolled her eyes at Ellis.

"Ellis, don't tease your sister. Besides, you should be happy she cares enough about you to mother you."

"Mom, where is Dad? He loves your blueberry pancakes. Why isn't he down for breakfast? Is he feeling well?"

"Your dad left very early this morning, Bray. Said he had something to take care of first thing this morning." Noel looked at her mother with concern.

"Mom, it's Saturday. What could Dad possibly have to do so early on a Saturday morning?"

"I bet I can guess."

"Ellis, come on, man, don't start, all right?"

"Actually, I'm glad it's just the four of us here right now. I need to discuss something with you guys." Noel laid her fork down and stared at her mother. Ellis kept eating his pancakes as if they'd run away from him if he didn't hurry up and finish them.

Bray reached over and touched his mother's hand before saying, "What's up, Mom? What's going on?"

"Your father's drinking, it's getting worse… Honestly, I don't know what to do about it. He won't even consider going to AA. Sometimes I think he feels his alcoholism is a joke. Every time I try to have a serious conversation with him about it, he just looks at me and laughs. Maybe it's his way of dealing with the problem…I don't know!"

"He is crazy!"

"Ellis, don't speak about your father that way, son. I've decided…a decision that I think is best for all of us." Waverly paused and tried to come up with the right words.

Noel shot a glance at Ellis, whom she felt was making an absolute pig of himself. "Ellis, is that your eighth pancake or tenth? Come up for air, will you?"

"Leave me alone, Noi. I let you eat all twenty of your pancakes in peace." Noel just shook her head at Ellis and turned her attention back to her mother.

"Mom, what? What have you decided?" Noel asked.

"I've given your father two months to do something about his drinking…and if he doesn't…I am going to leave him. We are going to leave him." Noel looked at her mother in disbelief.

LINDA MCCAIN

"What...Mom, you can't be serious! No! Leave Dad? No! Mom he is sick... How could you even consider leaving him at a time like this?" Bray looked at Noel.

"Noi, calm down."

"No, I won't calm down, Bray! Mom! Please! We're a family and you've always taught us that family should stick together, support each other! Now you are telling us that you are thinking of leaving Dad!"

Ellis drank the last of his orange juice and looked at his mother. "Mom, whatever you decide to do, I'm with you. I'm surprised you've put up with him this long. I'll see you guys later. I'm going for a run."

"Ellis, you come back here. This conversation isn't over," Noel shouted at him. Ellis kept walking, not even looking back.

"As soon as Mom finished speaking and telling us what she'd decided to do, Noi, the conversation was over for me. My mother's name is Waverly, not Noel." Ellis walked out of the room. Noel jumped up and ran upstairs, and Bray just sat there and stared down at his empty plate.

"Bray?"

"It's okay, Mom, I understand. I've got to get showered and dressed. I have to pick Dylan up in about an hour. I'll see you tonight." After Bray walked out of the kitchen, Waverly started clearing the table while wondering if she'd made the right decision to leave Nevin if it came to that.

Bray fell across his bed and pulled out his cell phone. He held the phone close to his ear, as if Waverly would walk in the room any minute and find him talking to his dad. Why this bothered him, he didn't know. Why he felt

118

he had to keep conversations with his dad a secret from his mom, he couldn't figure out.

Bray dialed Nevin's cell and hoped he'd answer. "Hey, Bray, what's going on, son? Everything all right?" Nevin asked after picking up on the fifth ring.

"Dad, that is the question I should be asking you. You were not at breakfast this morning. Mom made blueberry pancakes. You love those."

"Yeah, I know son. I had to leave early this morning. A lot going on at work, and I needed to get in and get started on a few things."

Bray held the phone to his ear and tried to think of how to ask his father a question that had been bothering him for a long time. "Bray, is there something else? Look, I've really got a lot going on here. Can we talk—"

"Dad, is everything all right with you and Mom?"

"What do you mean by that, son?"

"I don't know, it just seems like you two haven't really been talking lately, and again you were not at breakfast…"

"Bray, I just told you, I've got a lot going on at work and I needed to go in today for a bit, that's all. Don't try to read something into what's not there."

"I've decided to go to Northwestern University."

"That's great, Bray! You know I'm really proud of you, right?"

"I know, Dad. But I'll only go if…"

"If what?"

"If you promise me you will get some help." Nevin didn't say anything. "I mean it, Dad. If you don't promise me that you will make a serious effort to stop drinking, get some help, I'm not going."

"And what are you going to do, Bray? Throw away a fully paid scholarship? That's crazy!"

"No, Dad, what's crazy is that you are drinking yourself into an early grave and you won't try to do anything about it!"

"I've got to go, Bray. I'll talk to you tonight!" Bray stared at the phone after Nevin disconnected the call and then shut his eyes tight to lessen a pounding headache.

*****

"What about this color, you like it? I think black is hot! I mean, I know a lot of girls wouldn't think of wearing a black dress to their prom, but that's the point. It'll be unique, and this dress is nice!" Dylan looked at Bray. "Hey, did you hear what I just said?"

"Yeah, Dylan, I heard you," Bray said absentmindedly.

"Okay, you don't like the dress. Is it because it's black or you haven't even looked at it or heard a word I just said? What's wrong with you?"

"I'm sorry, the dress is great, Dylan, and you know I'd like you in anything you choose to wear."

"Okay, that's it! I'm putting this dress back for now and you and I are heading to the food court. I think you need to eat!"

"I'm not hungry."

"Well, I am, and you need to talk."

"About what?"

"About whatever it is that's intruding on my time with you."

Dylan and Bray found a table in a secluded area of the food court. After putting a little pepper on her pasta salad, she looked at Bray. "What's going on, Bray? Here, do you want half of my pasta salad, because I want half of your burger."

"Yeah, sure."

"I'm listening, what's up?"

"I may not be going to Northwestern University, Dylan." Dylan was about to take a bite of Bray's burger but didn't; she laid it back down instead.

"What are you talking about? You're making no sense!"

"My dad, I can't leave him in the fix he is in, Dylan, no way! I won't do it!"

"Bray!"

"He is my father, Dylan!"

"Exactly! He is your father, you're not his! You shouldn't have to babysit a grown man and throw your life away in the process!"

"I can't believe you just said that! How am I throwing my life away by trying to make sure my father is okay? How?" Dylan looked down at the table and then up at Bray with tears in her eyes.

"Bray…please? This is your future…*our* future we are talking about here. I'm sorry your dad is a…"

"Is a what? Just say it, Dylan… Is an alcoholic?"

Dylan pushed away from the table and got up. "Where are you going?"

"Excuse me, Bray, I need to go to the bathroom. I'll be right back. Eat your burger, it's getting cold."

"Dylan, are you all right? I'm sorry, I'm very sorry," Bray said while touching her on the arm.

"I'm fine, Bray, I just need to… I'll be right back… Eat your burger."

Bray looked down at his burger and then snatched it up, along with his fries, and threw them in the trash. He sat there fuming! "How could I ruin this day for Dylan, how could you do this to her? All she wanted to do was go shopping, pick out her prom dress, and get my approval." Bray sat there talking to himself, getting angrier and angrier!

When Dylan returned to the table, he stood up and pulled her onto his lap and then said softly to her, "I'm sorry, Dylan. I'm sorry, I didn't mean to ruin this for you. No more talking about my dad. No more, not today. Go over, sit down, and enjoy your pasta salad."

"What happened to your burger?"

"I tossed it in the trash!" Dylan looked at him, and they both laughed.

*****

Nevin sat at the bar and finished off a bottle of wine. He drank two glasses and then warned himself that he'd had enough. Still, two glasses turned into three, and before he knew it, he'd emptied the bottle. Reason warned him long before he finished the third glass not to, but desire made him turn it up to his mouth and drink until there was no more.

He'd noticed the attractive woman sitting on the stool beside him. She'd been staring at him for the last twenty minutes it seemed, and he'd tried to figure out why.

"Hello, do I know you from somewhere?" Nevin said casually.

The woman set her drink down and studied him for a second before saying, "No, but you definitely look like someone I'd like to get to know." Nevin smiled, picked up his cell phone, and sent Waverly a text full of misspelled words and incomplete sentences, trying to explain to her he was on his way home. "Are you ignoring me?" The woman asked as she glanced at Nevin.

"Yep, pretty much," he said as he reached in his wallet and handed Jasper, the bartender, money to pay for his bottle of wine.

"Nev, you okay, man? You gonna be able to make it home okay? You seem pretty wasted!"

"I may not be able to hold on to a buck, but I can certainly hold my alcohol." Jasper looked at him.

"Let me call someone to come get you, Nev."

"Nope, I'm good. I'll see you tomorrow." Jasper and the woman at the bar who was sitting next to Nevin followed him out the door with their eyes.

The woman took another sip of her drink and said, "He'll never make it."

It was seven-thirty by the time Nevin settled behind the wheel of his car. He was feeling a little sick to his stomach but ignored it and started the engine. He decided to take Lombar Road home, as it was quicker, he reasoned, and he felt he needed to get home fast before he lost his lunch right onto the floor of his car.

*****

At seven thirty-two, Bray dropped Dylan off. They were happy; Dylan had purchased the black dress for the prom and Bray a black tux with white shirt and tie to match. "Bray, you look tired. I'm sorry I kept you out so late. Why don't you take Lombar Road home? It's quicker from here and I don't want you on the road any later than you have to be at this point."

"Okay, cool, good idea. I am feeling a little tired." Dylan looked at Bray.

"I love you, Bray Berman."

"I love you too."

Dylan reached in on the driver's side and kissed Bray on the cheek. It was too hard to try and kiss him on the mouth with him sitting behind the wheel. "Text me as soon as you get in."

"Okay, I will. Good night!"

"Good night!"

Bray started the engine and pulled off. He was feeling good; although the day with Dylan at the mall started off a little rough, it ended great. He glanced at the clock in the car; it was seven forty-five. He turned on the radio and whistled to the sound of the song "Walk This Way" by Aerosmith.

*****

At seven forty-five, Nevin could feel himself losing control of the car as it began to swerve all over the road. He tried to sit up straight to clear his head, but he was losing the battle.

*****

Bray's cell phone rang; it was now seven-fifty, and Waverly was calling. "Hey, baby, you okay? You almost home? I was getting a little worried."

"Almost there, Mom. See you soon!"

"Okay, sounds good. Love you."

"Love you, too, Mom." Bray smiled to himself as he thought of Dylan and how much he cared about her, how he was looking forward to a bright future with her by his side.

At seven fifty-five, Bray looked up and noticed a car heading straight at him! "What the…" He laid on his horn, but the car kept coming at him at full speed. Bray blinked and glanced in the next lane over, trying to figure out if he could somehow force his way in between the cars bumper to bumper in that lane and saw that he couldn't! There was too much traffic and not enough room in between cars for him to even try to get over into the next lane. He panicked and laid on his horn repeatedly!

"Oh my god! Oh my god! It's Dad! That's Dad. I'd know his car anywhere! Dad, stop! Please! Dad!" Nevin hit Bray so hard that Bray's car flipped over.

*****

Nevin's car sped around in the middle of the street, almost colliding with traffic in the other lane! Nevin gripped the steering wheel and was somehow able to bring the car under control. His front bumper was hanging off, but he didn't care. He was still alive, he thought to himself!

When Nevin was able to pull off to the side of the road, he turned the car off and started cursing the traffic and trying to figure out what happened. "I must have hit a deer... Did a deer hit me?" He felt the warm ooze of blood running down his face and reached up to feel a small gash in his head. He was so drunk he didn't try to wipe the blood off. He started the car up and headed for the nearest emergency room, praying that he would be able to make it there.

*****

Dylan stepped out of the shower, grabbed her towel, and started drying off. Glancing at her cell phone that lay on her wicker clothes hamper, she asked herself, "Where is that boy? It's almost ten o'clock and he still hasn't texted me yet." After getting in bed and pulling the covers up under her chin, she sent Bray a text. "Bray???" She then turned over and tried to relax. Almost twenty minutes passed with no response from Bray. "Okay, now I'm getting upset."

Dylan picked up the phone and called him, and her call went straight to his voice mail. She stared at the phone and tried to figure out why he didn't answer her. Worry forced its way into her mind, although she fought to shut it out. Searching quickly through her list of contacts, she found Noel's cell number and called her, only to be met with the same outcome she had gotten after trying to reach Bray; the call went directly to Noel's voice mail. She called Ellis, TJ, and Jermaine, and the result was the same with each of them. No answer and call rolling to their voice mail. "What is going on? Bray! Something is wrong. I can feel it! Something is not right!"

Dylan jumped out of bed and ran to her mother's room, calling out to her as she did so. "Mom, Mom!" When she reached Cree's room, she snatched open the door only to find she wasn't there. Her hands started to shake she was getting so nervous. She stopped and took a deep breath, trying to calm her fears. "Stop it, stop it! He is fine, Bray is fine." She dialed Cree's number, no answer.

Struggling out of her pajamas as she ran to the bathroom, she tossed them to the floor and yanked the jeans and shirt she'd worn to the mall out of the wicker clothes hamper, put them on, and then ran back in her room and threw on flip-flops, picked up her cell phone, tossed it in her purse, and ran to her car. Her hands were shaking so much by now she couldn't get the key in the ignition. "Come on! Come on! What is wrong with this stupid key!" Finally, she gave up and rummaged through her bag, searching for her cell phone. She dug it out and called Bray again and again and again until she felt sick to her stomach with worry. Every time he didn't answer, it pushed her stress level up another notch. One more notch and she was sure she'd go insane.

Dylan felt drained—drained of energy, drained of determination. She started to realize that no matter how many times she called Bray, no matter how fast she got to him, it wouldn't change what had already happened, and something had, she knew it without a shadow of a doubt. Bray would never do this. He always, *always*, texted or called when he said he would. He never let her calls go to his voice mail, never! "Something is wrong with Bray," she said so low to herself that you would practically have to be in her mouth to hear what she'd said.

The sound of her cell phone ringing made Dylan jump; she was a structure of anxiety! As soon as she noticed her mother's number, she answered. "Mom, I can't reach him, I can't reach Bray! I can't reach Noi, Ellis, TJ, Jermaine, none of them! Mom, what's going on?"

Cree fought to keep her composure, she had to, or Dylan might wind up in the same situation Bray was in right now. "Dylan, I am on my way home. Where are you?"

"Mom…what? Why do you need to know where I am? Mom, where is he? Where is Bray! You know something and you're not telling me!"

Cree was in her car, driving as fast as she could, trying to get to Dylan before someone else did with the news of Bray's car accident. Tears blinded her vision, and heavy traffic made her want to get out and jog the rest of the way home. She was sure she'd get there faster! "I'm turning on to our street now, I'm almost there. Just stay where you are, Dylan."

Dylan whispered weakly, "I'm in my car."

Cree pulled into the driveway behind Dylan's car. She got out of her car slowly and walked up to the driver's side of Dylan's car. Dylan sat there, staring straight ahead. As soon as she looked up and noticed her mother, she started nodding her head back and forth slowly. "No...No, Mom! I don't want to know, I don't want to know!"

Cree tried to open Dylan's door, but it was locked. "Dylan, baby, open the door. Open your door, Dylan." Dylan didn't move. The window was halfway rolled down. Cree struggled to get her arm in and take the lock off herself, but the window wasn't down far enough. "Dylan! Open the door!" Still no response. Cree ran around to the passenger side of the car where the window was wound down a little further. She stuck her hand in the door and unlocked it. She then slid over as close as she could get to Dylan, pulled her into her arms, and held her as tightly as she could. Dylan looked up at her.

"Is he alive? Please, just tell me he is alive."

Chapter 11

Traffic on Lombar Road was backed up for miles. Police officers smothered the area. There was a police officer at the beginning and end of the road, while two other officers directed traffic to alternate routes. Drivers became restless, as many of them were tired from a long day of shopping, fussing with sleepy children and just wanting to get home. It was a Saturday night, and no one felt like sitting in traffic for the rest of the evening.

Officer Robbie McBride sat in his police cruiser and tried to make some sense of the accident. He was one of the first officers to arrive on the scene after the dispatcher radioed in the accident, saying a woman had phoned in an accident on Lombar Road and that one of the victims was pinned in his car. When he got there, he recognized the car but then thought to himself, *It can't be, it just couldn't be Waverly Berman's car*. He thought about calling his son Jermaine to see if Bray was with him. If so, he could ask Bray if his mother was home. He was trying to do everything but walk up to that flipped-over car and discover Waverly in it.

Robbie stood at a distance and stared at the car, trying to bring himself to approach it and learn who was in it. He rubbed his hands over his head and counted to ten, hoping this would rid him of the nauseating feeling in the bottom of his stomach. He closed his eyes and said, "Please, God." As he approached the car, he started to count again. He looked in the car. "Oh my god! Bray!"

*****

Noi glanced out the window, searching for some sign of Bray's car. Nevin had gotten in about an hour earlier with his head all bandaged up. "Dad, what happened to you?"

"Not now, Noi. I need to get to my bed." Noel's eyes followed him to his room. She then turned away from him while shaking her head and mumbling under her breath. "Why isn't Bray home yet?" Noel said softly to herself.

Waverly sat at the kitchen table and tried to figure out what was keeping Bray. After all, she had spoken to him much earlier, and he had said he was on his way home. What could be keeping him? she wondered.

Waverly started pacing back and forth. She thought about calling the hospital to see if there were any reported accidents. Cree was on duty tonight and she could speak directly to her. "No! I can't even begin to imagine that Bray has been in an accident," she said to herself. She walked up behind Noel, who was still looking out the window for Bray. "Any sign of your brother yet?" Noel let out a nervous sigh, turned, and looked at her mother.

"No."

"Have you tried calling Dylan?"

"No, Mom, it's late, and Dylan is probably asleep by now."

"She and Bray went to the mall earlier today, Noi. I know they did because Bray told me they were going."

Waverly and Noi turned toward the window as head-lights loomed in the distance and came closer and closer until they stopped at the edge of their driveway. Noi turned quickly and looked at her mother, her own heart racing. Ellis, who had been sitting on the sofa, trying to figure out where Bray could be after dialing his cell phone repeatedly, jumped up and rushed to the window.

The police officers got out. Robbie led the way as they walked to the door. He felt he needed to be the one to tell Bray's family about his car accident. He wanted to tell Jermaine but wasn't sure where he was and didn't want to chance upsetting him if he was somewhere on the road. Waverly opened the door. Robbie looked at her and tried to speak but couldn't. His partner stepped forward and mumbled a few words to her. Waverly looked at the officer and then fell to the floor.

When they got to the hospital, Noi and Ellis jumped out and ran inside. Nevin stayed behind and helped Waverly walk into the emergency room with difficulty. He was still feeling a little tipsy. Waverly felt her legs were about to fail her. When a nurse noticed her, she looked at her sadly. "Dr. Berman?"

"Where is he, where is my son? I…I said where is my son?"

"I'm sorry, I'm sorry. He is still being operated on. Dr. Berman, please have a seat."

Waverly stared at the nurse as if she was crazy, she had to be. How dare she, a nurse, tell her what to do. She was the doctor and she was the one who gave orders. How dare she tell her to sit down. Besides, she was Bray's mother. If anyone could take care of and save her son, she could. Doesn't the nurse realize this? Waverly continued to carry on an irrational mental conversation with herself until Nevin led her over to a seat and helped her sit down.

Three hours later, Waverly sat in the hospital chapel clinging to a Bible so hard the knuckles on her hands were red. She looked at her hands, hands that had operated on patients, saved lives, and quieted the fears of family members with just a simple touch of reassurance. Yet there she sat, praying and holding onto a Bible instead of an operating instrument. There she sat, praying that somehow her son would pull through his operation and walk out the doors of Simon Memorial Hospital one day.

*****

Jermaine raced to the hospital, his heart pounding so loudly it drowned out the noise of the radio he'd turned on to try and keep him from falling apart. The silence was killing him. He needed noise, lots of it!

He'd been in bed when Noel called him. She was hysterical, and he could only make out some of what she was trying to tell him until he told her to calm down and then try to explain what was going on. Before she could finish telling him about Bray being in a car accident, Jermaine had jumped out of bed and was racing around his room with his cell phone in one hand and trying to pull on some clothes at the same time with the other hand. "Where, Noi! Where! What hospital!" That was all Jermaine could remember asking her before he jumped in his truck and headed for Simon Memorial Hospital at breakneck speed!

*****

Noel walked into the chapel, feeling weak and help-less. Her mind and heart yearned to change the events of the previous hours. Start at the beginning of the day, from the point of her family all sitting around at breakfast that morning and enjoying her mother's blueberry pancakes. Bray wasn't in a hospital operating room fighting for his life. He was having breakfast with his family and sharing the news with them of his decision to go to Northwestern University and looking forward to shopping with Dylan at the mall later that afternoon. How did the day turn into her and her mom sitting in a hospital chapel praying to a god she'd never prayed to a day in her life before to please let Bray live?

Prayer, Noel pondered over the word, it's meaning. She didn't even know how to pray. All she knew was that when something very bad happened, people always mentioned prayer. Bray, lying in that operating room with so many tubes running through his body she'd lost count of them, was more than bad. It was horrific! She'd followed a nurse to Bray's operating room without notice after hearing her say that's where she was headed. She had to see him, she had to see Bray for herself, and once she had, she wished she hadn't. She had almost passed out!

"Mom?" Waverly turned and looked at Noel but said nothing. If whatever words she uttered weren't a plea for her son's life, then she had nothing to say. "Mom, Bray is out of surgery now. The doctor came out and asked to speak to us…together, to speak to Bray's family." Waverly didn't move. "Mom, we have to go now. We have to go find out how Bray is doing. We have to…"

"You go, Noi, go on, honey. I'll be there." Noi stared at her mother.

"I'm not going without you. We go together, or I don't go. I'm not leaving you here."

"How did you know I was here?"

"Dad told me. He said you said you needed to get to the hospital chapel."

Waverly closed her eyes and stood up, gripping the back of the bench in front of her for support. She laid the Bible down on the bench where she'd just sat and looked down at it. Suddenly it was as if the minute she put it down, what little strength she had left eased out of her body, leaving her powerless to deal with Bray's accident.

"Come on, Mom, it's okay. You can do this, just move. That's all you have to do is move." Waverly took a deep breath and grabbed Noel's hand, allowing her to guide her out of the hospital chapel. Noel took her hand away and put her arm around Waverly's waist, gently guiding her toward the door of the chapel. Waverly stopped. "Mom, what is it? Come on, we are almost at the door, come on."

"No." Noel quickly looked around for someone to help get Waverly to the door and out of it, but there was no one.

"Bray needs you. He needs you, Mom. He needs to see you. How will he ever know you are here if you don't walk out of this chapel? Now come on, just say a little prayer and move. Just move, Mom…please." Waverly didn't want to move; she wanted to plant herself right in the chapel until she'd been miraculously given the assurance that Bray was all right, that she would walk out of there and he be standing on the opposite side of the door waiting on her, wearing the same smile on his face he did when he told her he'd decided to go to Northwestern University this morning.

Dr. Kerry Monroe stood in front of Nevin and Ellis, speaking softly to them as Waverly and Noel approached them. "Kerry," Waverly said as she approached him. He was no stranger to her. The two of them had performed numerous surgeries together, and she also knew he was a specialist, an excellent doctor.

In all his years of practicing medicine, never once had he been in the position of having to inform a fellow doctor about the condition of a family member. He looked at Waverly, her husband, her son, and her daughter. He'd give anything to be able to wish this night away, to erase it from reality. "Waverly, may I please speak to you alone for a minute?"

"No, you may not. We stand before you as a family, Bray's family. *We* are his support system, not just me. So whatever you have to say, just say it, Kerry. Say it to all of us."

Kerry let out a nervous sigh. "The surgery went surprisingly well. However, Bray has a broken arm and several internal injuries. The police said his car was flipped over when they pulled him from the wreckage. When the car flipped over, it seems Bray must have landed on his back. There are several lacerations to his back, deep lacerations that took some time to stitch." Kerry paused and looked up at the ceiling. "Waverly, please, I need to speak with you alone."

Waverly stared at him before saying, "And go on, finish what you have to say."

Waverly knew the worst about Bray's accident was about to be revealed. Call it intuitiveness, whatever! She knew the tragic truth was about to be uttered whether she liked it or not. She braced herself. "Kerry, finish it now."

"Bray has injuries to his spinal cord...he..." Kerry became filled with emotion and he fought hard to conceal it, but he was losing the battle. This was a seventeen-year-old kid he was talking about. He knew Bray, knew he was a good kid, knew he was the star basketball player at Raymond DeMassi High known as Hoop. Waverly talked about him at every opportunity. Kerry felt like a father to him in some ways.

"Kerry, are you telling me my son...my son is going to be paralyzed?"

"Waverly, it's still a little too soon to tell. I just want to prepare you..."

"Prepare me? You're kidding, right? Kerry, you and I both know there is absolutely no way to prepare a family for the news that their loved one may be paralyzed."

"Partial paralysis, Waverly," Kerry said sympathetically. Waverly laughed to herself.

"Partial paralysis, and that's supposed to make it easier to accept?"

For the first time for some odd reason, Waverly looked at Nevin, who'd started to cry, and said, "What happened to your head?" Nevin just shook his head slowly and wiped away his tears. He honestly couldn't remember what happened to his head at the moment.

"I don't know. I think I may have hit a deer on the way home." They all looked at him strangely. Ellis shook his head and walked out of the hospital. Noel ran to the bathroom; she felt she was about to be sick. Jermaine, who had been standing in the distance and heard every word concerning Bray's condition, turned around and walked back out of the hospital.

*****

Cree sat at the edge of Dylan's bed, where Dylan had sobbed her eyes out and cried herself to sleep no matter how hard Cree tried to console her. She'd tried to come up with every scenario possible to gently tell Dylan about Bray's car accident. After realizing there was no perfect scenario to help her explain that Bray had been rushed to the emergency room with several injuries and incoherent, Cree told her as gently as possible about the accident and that Bray was in the emergency room undergoing surgery. Dylan had just stared at her at first and said more so to herself than to Cree, "I knew it. I knew something was terribly wrong."

When Cree had seen that it was Bray being rushed into the hospital, she'd let out a scream that belied her reputation of being a strong doctor, a doctor with the reputation of being controlled under the worst medical emergencies. The emergency room staff had been alerted that a car accident victim was being rushed in and to the seriousness of his condition.

As they rushed Bray to the emergency room, Cree had run behind them. She'd tried to run into the operating room, even though she wasn't suited up properly. All she could think about was helping Bray. The nurse on duty had noticed her. "Dr. Hayes, you can't be in here like that. You're not suited up." The nurse also knew that Bray was Dr. Berman's son and Cree was a very close friend of hers. After the nurse rushed over and quickly whispered something to Dr. Kerry Monroe, he turned sharply from working on Bray and yelled at Cree to wait outside the operating room. Reluctantly Cree obeyed, turned, and walked out of the room. Just as she did so, Dylan came to mind.

"Dylan, oh my god! I've got to get to Dylan before someone else does with the news of Bray's accident." She'd rushed over to the nurse's station and told them she had an emergency and needed to leave and then asked them to contact the doctor on standby for the night.

Chapter 12

Nevin opened the door to Robbie and looked at him as if he carried a plague. "Come on, man, don't look at me like that."

"Come on, Robbie, Bray hasn't really gotten used to being home from the hospital yet. I mean, give it a break, why don't you? You were just here it seems."

"May I come in?" Nevin hesitated. "Please?"

"Robbie, look, I know you are a police officer and you're just doing your job, but…"

"Hello, Officer McBride," Bray said as he wheeled himself into the living room. Robbie looked at Bray and then at his wheelchair. He still couldn't believe it. He still could not believe that Bray was one day getting ready to go off to Northwestern University and the next confined to a wheelchair. He coughed nervously.

"Hey, Bray, how are you doing, man?"

"I'm okay. Jermaine just left. He went to pick us up some tacos for lunch. He knows they are my favorite."

"Bray, I know this is difficult and I know you answered a year's worth of questions while you were in the hospital, but I can't let this rest, Bray. I can't leave it alone, not even for a day or two without it driving me crazy. Jermaine, he is constantly asking questions, wanting to know if we are any closer to finding the person who hit you on Lombar Road that night."

Bray wheeled himself up closer to Robbie and his dad. "I've told you all I can about the night of the accident. What else do you want?"

"I want to find the person who hit you and wring his neck! That's what I want! But since I'm a police officer, I'll have to settle for just finding and arresting him or her." Robbie paused. "I need your help to do this, Bray. I need you to try as hard as you can to come up with a description of the car that hit you that night and resulted in you being in that wheelchair."

Bray looked down and said, "I'm sorry, but as I just said, I've told you all I can about that night."

"All you can or all you're willing to tell, Bray. Son, I feel there is something you're not telling me."

"Hold on, Robbie, if Bray said he is telling you all he can about that night, then he is telling you all he can! Just let it go for now! Bray is still trying to get his strength back."

"Nevin, you need to understand that the more time that is allowed to pass without us finding the person who hit Bray, the less likely it is that we will ever find them. We have reason to believe that whoever hit Bray that night was intoxicated. There were swerve marks all over the road."

"Excuse me, Dad, Officer McBride, I have something I need to take care of in my room. It was nice to see you, Officer McBride."

"Bray, you know you don't have to call me Officer McBride. I'm your best friend's dad."

"Yeah, I know. Thank you. Please excuse me."

"Sure, son," Nevin said and watched his son wheel himself back to his room.

"It was a nice graduation, don't you think, Robbie? I can't believe our children have finally graduated from high school."

"How are you coming along with the drinking, Nevin?"

"What kind of question is that, Robbie? I was talking to you about the graduation. Where did that question come from?"

"I've had to pull you over once or twice for driving under the influence. It's a reasonable question, Nevin. I just want to know how you're coming along with AA visits."

"I'm not going to AA."

"Maybe you should be, especially considering what just happened to your son. I'm convinced that whoever hit Bray that night was drunk." Nevin looked at Robbie.

"It was good to see you, Robbie. Good night."

"Good night, Nevin."

Nevin closed the door behind Robbie and then walked to the middle of the floor and stood in thought. "Why is Bray having such a hard time remembering that night he was hit head-on on Lombar Road?" Like Robbie, he'd questioned him almost every day, and every day Bray gave him the same answer he'd just given Robbie; it was almost as if it was rehearsed. "I've told you everything I can about that night," was his answer every time.

Nevin knocked softly on Bray's door. "Hey, son, you need anything? Is it time for your meds?"

"No, Dad. Mom helped me with them before leaving for the grocery store. Hey, you want to come in, play a game of cards before Jermaine gets here with the tacos?" Nevin walked over and sat down on the edge of Bray's bed.

"Son, I need to ask you something."

"Dad, look, I'm really tired. Maybe I should try to get some rest."

"But you just asked me if I wanted to play a game of cards."

"I know, I'm sorry but I'm starting to feel a little weak. I'm going to take a nap."

"Okay, son, okay. Do you want me to help you onto the bed?"

"No thanks, I'm good. I'm just going to take a quick nap in the chair. Besides, Jermaine will be here soon. When he gets here, will you please just ask him to come on back to my room?" Nevin stood and let out a heavy sigh.

"Sure, son, I'll do that. You get some rest now."

"Thanks, Dad."

Bray rolled his wheelchair up closer to his window. He could see the basketball court that he, his dad, and Ellis had put up in the backyard when his parents first bought the house. He loved his house. It was beautiful, although not very big. There were four bedrooms, and he remembered his father arguing for a house that had at least five bedrooms. He smiled as he remembered Waverly's argument against it: "Four bedrooms is more than enough for this family. I don't want to live in a museum, I want to live in a home. Besides, there are some people who don't even have one bedroom, so be grateful."

"I will never forget those words," Bray said softly to himself. He strained his neck to get a closer view of the basketball court, which enabled him to also get a glimpse of the lake and the backyard. *Mom argued against a fifth bedroom but not against the large backyard and the big beautiful lake behind it.* The sound of Jermaine's knock on his bedroom door interrupted his thoughts.

"Hey, what's up? I got the tacos you wanted. All chicken, right?"

"Yep," Bray said as he turned his chair away from the window. Jermaine started taking the food out of the bag and glanced at Bray.

"What's up, Bray? What's going on, man? You feeling okay?"

"Yeah, J, I'm fine. I had my last physical therapy session yesterday, and they said I did great. Plus, I feel great, so it's all good!"

"All right, just so you're good, that's all I care about. I also picked you up some of those chips you like, with extra salsa!"

"Hey, now that's what's up! Thanks, J!"

"Anything for you, Bray," Jermaine said as he handed him his food and drink.

They were both quiet for a while as they ate their food. Jermaine emptied his bottled water and leaned back on Bray's bed. "I saw my dad leaving… So what's going on? Any word on the progress of finding who hit you that night?" Bray stuck the rest of his last taco in his mouth, leaned back, and, as if he was trying to make a three-point shot on the court, threw the wrapper at the trash can across the room, and the wrapper went right in the can.

"Awesome! You still got it, Bray!" Bray smiled.

"Well, at least I'd like to think so!"

"So did my dad have any news, good news, like they found the… I can't say what I want to say, Bray, because it is too disgusting, even for my ears. Anyway! Any word?"

"J, I'm really not up for conversation regarding the accident right now."

Jermaine sat up on the bed and exhaled loudly. "What's going on, Bray? What are you holding on to? Why is it that every time me or anyone else asks you about the accident, you never want to talk about it? Don't internalize it, Bray. If you do, it will kill you, I'm telling you!" Bray didn't say anything. "Bray, do you know who hit you head-on that night on Lombar Road? Are you trying to protect someone?"

"Let it go, J! Let it go already!" Bray yelled at him. Jermaine got up off the bed and walked over to look out the window, his back turned to Bray.

"Let it go? Bray, you are talking to the wrong person if that's what you want because I will never let it go! I will never let it go, Bray! I will not *rest* until I find out who did this to you! They took your life away from you, Bray, your life!"

"Jermaine, I'm still here, I'm still alive! I'm still going to become a writer. I'll be taking writing classes online! I'm going to be okay, J!"

Jermaine turned away from the window to look at Bray and, with tears in his eyes, said, "Well, I'm not, not until I find the person who did this to you! And even then, how I feel from this day forward, having to see you in that wheelchair, is questionable."

Bray tried to change the subject. "Hey, J, it's exciting, man. You will be leaving for Harvard in the fall! That's awesome! This is what you waited for, J, your dad worked so hard and saved for!" Jermaine walked back over and sat down on the bed. He looked down at the floor.

"I'm not going, Bray, I'm not going to Harvard now." Bray looked at him, confused, and then rolled his wheelchair over to him.

"Not going? What do you mean, J? You've got to go! You've worked so hard for this, kept your grades up! Your dad has worked harder than anyone I know to save up for this and you're not going? J, that's insane! What's up?"

Jermaine looked up at Bray. "I'm not leaving you, Bray, I'm not going. I'm staying here and going to Virginia School of Law. It's only about five miles away from Taverston. This way I can drive there and back every day and be home still." Bray just looked at him; he couldn't believe what he was hearing.

"J...?"

"That's it, Bray, end of discussion! I'm not going. I am staying right here. I'm going to be here to help you when needed to go to the doctor or your meds picked up or for anything you need, even if it's just to talk. I'm going to be here for you, Bray."

"Jermaine, I can't let you do this, I won't!"

"Oh yeah, and how are you going to stop me? What are you going to do, jump up out of that wheelchair and kick my butt?" They both laughed.

"That's not funny, J."

"Hey, but it made us laugh!"

"Seriously, Jermaine! You have the potential to become a great lawyer someday. Don't throw your chances away because of me. I don't want that, J."

"Bray, the college I attend is not going to secure my chances of becoming a great lawyer. My grades, efforts, and passing the bar will! If I apply myself in my classes and keep my straight A streak going, I'll make it, Bray. I will become a lawyer. Besides, this small town of ours could use a good lawyer." Jermaine smiled and walked over to toss his trash from the tacos in the can.

"Jermaine?"

"That's the end of it, Bray. I've already applied to Virginia School of Law. Just waiting to hear from them." Bray looked at Jermaine out of the corner of his eye.

"Have you told your dad?"

"Not yet, plan to tonight."

"Jermaine, you can't do this!"

"You don't want to discuss your accident, I'm down with that...for now. I don't want to discuss my decision to stay here and attend Virginia School of Law, so hey, we are even. Let's find something else to argue about, like that talkative girlfriend of yours. Where is she on a Sunday afternoon?"

"She is coming over tonight. She was here until almost eleven thirty last night. I think I may have upset her." Jermaine looked at him, confused.

"Yeah, what happened?"

"I don't really want to talk about it. When she texted me this morning, I told her to stay in and rest and just come over tonight."

After Jermaine left, Bray pulled out his cell phone and sent Waverly a text. "Hey, Mom, you okay? You've been gone for a while and I was just wondering if you'd found everything okay at the store?" Bray waited for Waverly's response; a minute hadn't even passed and he was on pins and needles.

Ever since the accident, he'd fallen into the habit of checking on his family if any of them showed up late for dinner or if Noi and Ellis didn't come in from school on time. If his dad hadn't made it in to work on time by the time he called him that morning. His accident had him on edge; he even checked on Jermaine and Dylan if he didn't hear from them at least twice a day. He was terrified that someone he loved would wind up like him and he just couldn't handle that.

"Hey, you!"

"Hey, Mom, I just sent you a text! Where were you? What took you so long at the store? You left over an hour ago!" Waverly closed the door and walked over to sit on Bray's bed.

"I'm sorry, baby, the store was crowded. I was trying to find that ice cream you like, but the first store I went to didn't have it, so I tried a second one not far from it, and guess what, I got it!" Bray smiled.

"Thanks, Mom."

"Sure, son… Bray, your dad and I have been doing some thinking and talking. Maybe…?"

"Maybe what, Mom?"

"Bray, we would like for you to see someone. We think…?"

"You think I need to see a psychiatrist, is that what you are trying to say."

"No, honey, no, that's not it at all," Waverly rushed to say. "Just a counselor, Bray, it could even be someone your own age, someone who has or is experiencing the same thing you're going through."

"I'm okay, Mom, I don't need to see anyone." Waverly didn't say anything right away; she just got up and started to straighten out the covers on Bray's bed.

"Okay, son. Dinner will be ready in a few hours. I'll be in shortly before to help you get washed up." Waverly looked around the room and noticed Bray's basketball trophies lined up so neatly on his bookshelf. She wanted to walk over to them, pick them all up, and throw them against the wall, one by one.

"Mom?" Bray's voice snapped Waverly out of her thoughts.

"Yes, Bray, what is it, son?"

"When are you going back to work? I think you need to get back to work."

"My leave of absence isn't up for another month. I was given two months of approved leave to care for you, thanks to Cree's help. Cree is handling my patients. And what I need isn't to get back to work, Bray. What I need is to beat the crap out of whoever put you in that chair. Get some rest, son. I'll be back later."

*****

Dylan sat up in bed and gripped her stomach. "Oh my god, if I throw up one more time, I'm going to lose the lining of my stomach." Dylan had been throwing up ever since she came in from Bray's house last night. She'd had to tiptoe to the bathroom so Cree wouldn't hear her. Grateful that Cree had left for work, she released a sigh of relief. "What is wrong with me?" As she felt another bout of nausea coming on, she jumped up and ran to the bathroom. She fell on the floor and leaned her head over the stool until her rush of nausea was emptied into the toilet.

"I'm not going back to bed. What is the point? I'll only wind up right back where I am in less than five minutes." She tried to make herself throw up more, once she'd finally stopped, wanting to get it all out once and for all, but nothing would come. Suddenly, she felt yet another wave of nausea and she tried to get it out, and still nothing would come. She had the dry heaves. Dylan stumbled to the bathroom sink and rinsed her mouth out, then pulled her towel down and spread it out beside the stool, and then lay on it. She didn't have the energy to drag herself back to bed. "I could die right here. I am in this house all alone and I can't even make it back to my cell phone right now. God, please don't let me die," she said weakly. She drifted off to sleep, and when she woke up, Cree was kneeling beside her and calling her name.

"Dylan! Dylan, honey, wake up," Cree said while gently shaking her to help wake her.

Dylan stirred but didn't wake up. Cree put her hand to Dylan's forehead and then jumped up and ran to the kitchen and brought her back a glass of water mixed with a little lime juice and sugar. She saw that she had been throwing up.

"Dylan, wake up. Wake up and take a sip of this drink." Dylan slowly opened her eyes and looked up at Cree.

"Mom, I didn't hear…"

"It's okay, honey. I walk softly sometimes."

"What time is it?"

"It's a little after four. Let's get you up off the floor. What's going on? Are you sick? Did you pass out?" Dylan tried to help Cree get her up off the floor, but she was so weak she was of very little help.

"I can't believe I've been in here so long."

"How long have you been here on the floor like this?"

"It's been hours."

"Lie back down, Dylan. Lie back down and continue to sip on the drink. Can you hold onto the glass while I get something out of the medicine cabinet?" Dylan nodded her head yes and gripped her stomach before taking the glass from Cree's hand. Cree quickly reached in the medicine cabinet and pulled out baking soda. "Here, honey, let me pour this in your drink." Cree poured a little of the baking soda in the water, took the glass from Dylan, and shook the glass to help dissolve the baking soda. "Okay, drink this." Dylan tried to push the glass away and gripped her stomach again. "Dylan, drink it. That's an order."

"Mom, what is this? It smells awful!"

"Just drink it. I'm your mother and I'm a doctor. I think it's safe to trust me on this one." Dylan still wasn't convinced the drink was safe and looked at it. "Dylan, it's just a little lime juice, sugar, and baking soda mixture. Now drink it, please. It will quiet your nausea."

Dylan tried to take the glass from Cree and drink the mixture, but she was having trouble gripping it. "That's okay, Dylan, let me do it. I'll hold the glass while you drink." Dylan tried to get the drink down, but she gagged and coughed in the process, causing some of it to come flying out of her mouth and onto Cree's blouse. "That's okay, Dylan, that's okay, honey. At least, you got some of it down. You should start to feel better in a little while. Lie back down now. I'm going to run you a warm bath."

After Cree finished running Dylan's bath, helped her pull off her soiled clothes, and settled her into the tub, she looked at her. "Dylan, lay your head back and try to relax a little before you start to bathe, okay? I'm going to your room to strip your bed and change your sheets. I won't be long. I'll be right back! Right back, okay?" Dylan just nodded her head in acknowledgment and laid her head on the back of the tub.

Cree rushed to the linen closet and pulled out clean sheets for Dylan's bed and a bottle of Lysol spray. It was cool and breezy outside, so she cracked her window to let some fresh air in. After spraying the Lysol and running the vacuum cleaner over her carpet, Cree started to strip Dylan's bed.

When Cree yanked the covers from Dylan's bed, her journal fell to the floor. Cree looked at it and started to ignore it, but she tossed the covers to the floor and opened it. While leafing quickly through the journal, she squashed the guilt of invading Dylan's privacy while thinking opportunities like this came once in a lifetime so she'd better take advantage of it. Cree glanced toward the bathroom to make sure Dylan wasn't trying to make it back to her room and catch her reading the journal.

"Dylan, you okay?" Cree yelled to her as extra assurance that Dylan was still in the tub and that she was not at risk of being caught reading her journal.

"I'm okay."

"Great, I'll be right there." Looking at the last entry in Dylan's journal, she noticed it was dated for yesterday. She felt horrible for snooping, something she swore she would never do, but for some reason, she had to know what the entry was about, so she read it.

> Sometimes I wonder what Bray is really feeling, he is so distant. I try so hard to reach him, but he continues to shut me out. I tried to touch his hand, but he pulled back from me. It really hurt me to think he no longer wants me to touch him. I'm finding this very hard to understand. I still love him so much. I asked him if he still plans to marry me… He said no. I asked him why, he looked at me and said, "Things are different now, Dylan." I just stared at him for a second and then slowly turned and walked out of his house, got in my car, and drove home.

"Mom, what's keeping you? I'm done bathing now and I need help getting out of the tub, please." Cree brushed away a tear, quickly closed the journal, and laid it on Dylan's nightstand. "Coming, honey, I'll be right there. Just let me finish making up your bed."

Once Cree helped Dylan make it out of the tub and helped dry her off and put on a clean pair of pajamas, she walked her to her bedroom and helped her climb in bed. While pulling up the covers around her, she looked at her sadly, and Dylan noticed. "Mom, what's wrong?" Cree shook her head in response out of fear her voice would fail her. She gathered her emotions and said, "It's nothing, I'm fine. How are you feeling? Any better?"

"Yeah, I am. Thank you."

"You're welcome. You relax, I'm just going to get an extra pillow from my room to put behind your head to elevate you a little more, okay?"

"Okay."

Cree propped the pillow up behind Dylan's head and tried to elevate her as much as possible. "Would you like some ginger ale? Do you think you can keep it down?"

"Thanks, but I don't feel much like eating or drinking anything right now."

"I understand. When was the last time you tried to eat something?"

"I think…I think it was this morning."

"Did it stay down when you ate it?"

"No, not really."

"All right, okay…you get some rest now. I'm going to shower and try to get a little rest myself. Just call me if you need me."

"Thanks, Mom."

"Sure, honey."

Just as Cree started to pull Dylan's bedroom door closed, Dylan said, "Mom, would you please call Bray's mom and ask her to let him know I won't make it over? I was supposed to go over, but I'm not feeling well."

"Of course, I'll do it right now."

"Thanks."

"You get some rest now."

*****

Waverly opened Bray's bedroom door and stuck her head in. "Cree just called, said Dylan isn't feeling well and will not be coming over this evening." Bray hesitated before answering.

"Thanks, I'll text her later."

"Why don't you just call her, son?"

"I said I'll text her." Waverly looked at him for a second.

"Bray, is everything all right? You and Dylan okay?"

"Yep, perfect! Just perfect!" Waverly looked at him, trying to figure out what was really going on.

"Well, okay. Dinner is ready. I'm here Bray, always. Would you like me to help you wash up for dinner?" Bray didn't respond. "Please come on to the table now son, dinner is ready," Waverly said. Still no response from Bray. Waverly looked at him for a second longer, then slowly closed the door behind her and walked to the kitchen to join the others for dinner.

Bray wheeled himself up to the side of the table that had been cleared especially for him so his wheelchair would fit comfortably at it. Everyone was there except Nevin. "Where's Dad?"

"I don't know, Bray. Maybe he is working late, son. Don't you worry, help your plate with food. I made all your favorites tonight." Bray leaned back in his wheelchair and closed his eyes. They all looked at him.

"Bray, you okay? Are you in pain?" Noel asked.

Just then, the front door opened and Nevin walked in. Bray looked at him and let out a sigh of relief. "He is actually sober."

"Ellis!"

155

"It's okay, Waverly. Ellis is a growing boy. Unfortunately, his brain hasn't caught up with his age yet, but it will get there," Nevin said. Ellis looked down at his plate and said nothing.

"Dad, we are so glad you're here! This is the first time we've all been together for dinner since…" Noel looked around the table at her family before continuing, "since the accident. It feels nice."

"Noi, grab your father a plate from the kitchen, please, while he washes up for dinner."

"Sure, Mom!"

"Bray, how are you feeling, son?"

"I'm doing great, Dad! I just finished getting set up to take some online writing classes. I'm excited, can't wait to start!"

"That's great, son. I…I have two tickets here. I figured you and I could take in a movie tonight after dinner. You up for that?"

"Yeah! Thanks, Dad!"

"Movie starts at seven. We can take my new car."

"Okay, sounds great!"

"Dad, you never said what happened to your old car, why you decided to trade it in."

"Well, that night when I hit that deer on Lombar Road, it messed my car up more than I realized. It was on its last leg anyway, so I decided to trade it in for something new Noi."

"Lombar Road? Bray, isn't that the road your accident happened on?"

"Ellis, please, let's just enjoy our dinner. Like Noi said, it's nice to have us all here together for dinner."

*****

Dylan picked up her cell phone and scrolled down the contacts until Bray's name stared back at her. She'd just seen him yesterday, but still she missed him terribly. She thought about sending him a text. Under normal circumstances, she wouldn't have to think about sending him a text, she'd just do it. But they were no longer under normal circumstances, and she was beginning to wonder if anything between them would ever be or feel normal again.

She laid her cell phone back down on her nightstand and noticed her journal. "How did that get there? I thought it was in my bed. I remember tossing it beside me on top of the covers after I'd written in it last night. Mom must have put it there when she was stripping my bed. I don't know, the way I was feeling when I finished writing in it, I may have forgotten where I put it." Dylan pulled open the drawer to her nightstand, took out the remote to her television, and flipped through the channels until she found something worth watching.

Chapter 13

Waverly gently placed the spirea into the hole filled with Miracle-Gro soil and then covered the hole surrounding her newly planted shrub with the dirt she'd dug from the spot. Leaning back, she stretched, and her body felt achy and she knew exactly why. It wasn't from the gardening she'd gotten up early that morning to do. It was from days of helping Bray in and out of his chair to get in the tub or in bed. She and Nevin were about to lose their mind trying to come up with easier ways to help maneuver Bray so he could partake in the necessities of life—bathing, getting in bed, going to the various doctors.

Even though her job was a lucrative one and Nevin certainly made enough money to more than care for his family, Bray's medical bills, even with insurance, put a monumental hole in their family savings account. She so wanted to hire a nurse to help with the care of Bray, but after going over last night's budget for the household, she just didn't see how it was possible.

She got up off the ground with a small outcry of pain. She was achy to the point of wanting to get back down on the ground and just lie there until someone came out and found her there and then carried her inside. But there was much to be done. She picked up the bags of potting soil and gardening tools and put them in the shed. She then walked over and turned on the hose and watered the spirea she'd just planted. When she finished watering, she walked in the house to the bathroom and showered.

Waverly had just finished tossing a salad and making iced tea for Bray's lunch when the doorbell rang. She picked up the dishcloth and wiped her hands on it before walking swiftly to the door to open it. Ms. Purlasky and Megan greeted her with a big smile. "Ms. Purlasky, Megan, what?" Ms. Purlasky rushed up to Waverly and put a hand on both sides of Waverly's face and kissed her on each cheek. Then as if she lived there, Ms. Purlasky walked past Waverly and into the living room with two large shopping bags. Megan shot a quick glance at her mother, a little embarrassed.

"Mommy, we haven't been invited in yet."

"Come, Megan, bring the bags quickly!" Waverly stepped to the side so Megan could walk past her. She didn't know what to say or think.

"The kitchen, my dear, where is it?" Ms. Purlasky asked while looking around the room. Before Waverly could answer her, Ms. Purlasky stopped suddenly and looked down at the carpet. "My dear, when was the last time this carpet benefited from a good vacuuming? Actually, I think it's seen its best days. We must pull it up." Waverly's mouth fell open, and she put her hands on her hips and stared at Ms. Purlasky.

"Mommy, you can't say things like that to people in their own home! You can't say things like that to people, period."

"Well, it's the truth. Now come, Megan, stop idling."

Waverly followed Ms. Purlasky and Megan to the kitchen, still trying to figure out what they were doing there. What was going on? "So I spoke to Dr. Hayes last night. I practically had to twist her arm to get your address out of her. I had to bribe her, I promised to make her a pumpkin pie. I made her one and took it to the hospital after I'd recovered from my angioplasty. She loves my pumpkin pie, no surprise. Everybody loves my pumpkin pie. Why not? It's the best! I had to promise I'd make her two before she would give me your address. I got Cree's phone number from Kerry, my soon-to-be son-in-law. Show Dr. Berman your engagement ring, Megan!" Megan's face evolved into a huge grin before she stuck out her hand to show Waverly her engagement ring that almost blinded her. The diamond was so huge and sparkled from the rays of sunshine that lit up the kitchen. Waverly gasped and took Megan's hand to have a closer look at the ring.

"Megan, it's absolutely stunning! Oh, I am so happy for you and Kerry. Congratulations! Wow, I didn't even know you guys were dating!"

"Thank you, Dr. Berman. Thank you so much! Kerry and I started dating a little after Mom had her procedure. I know it seems a little too soon, but when it's right, you know it's right. Kerry is so good to me and Mommy. I really love him."

"Well, I'm very happy for you and Kerry."

"Okay, enough of that," Ms. Purlasky said as she started to take food from the shopping bags. "Sit down, Dr. Berman, and point to where all the pots, pans, and kitchen utensils are. Hopefully I will be able to see past all this clutter to where you're pointing to."

"Mommy!"

"Oh, shush, Megan! Dr. Berman knows what I'm saying is true. That's all right, though, because before you and I leave here today, Megan, Dr. Berman will not recognize her own home." Waverly pulled out a chair, sat down, and started pointing to the cabinets and where the cooking utensils were. She was too shocked and honestly too tired to put up a fight.

"Hello!" Ms. Purlasky stopped pulling out a baking pan and looked at Bray as he wheeled himself into the kitchen. She set the pan down on the counter and walked slowly over to Bray. "There he is, our boy, our *beautiful* boy." Ms. Purlasky looked Bray over. "God has blessed you with the beauty compared to that of Absalom. Not even that wheelchair can detract from your handsome face and features," Ms. Purlasky said as she walked up and stood in front of Bray with a smile on her face.

"Look, Megan, look at our boy, our Bray." Megan looked at Bray as her mother asked, and mentally agreed that he was an exceptionally handsome young man. Bray looked at Ms. Purlasky and then at his mother.

"You are wondering how I know your name. Yes, I know your name, son, I know a lot about you. Dr. Hayes, she has told me so many wonderful things about you. I've prayed for you day and night and I will continue to do so. You are going to do well in life. No car accident is going to hinder you from succeeding at whatever you want to accomplish in life, son. You are an achiever, I can see it in your eyes."

Bray looked at Ms. Purlasky and then at Megan; he'd never seen a more beautiful woman in his life. Megan was exquisite, Bray thought. He could see why Dr. Monroe had wasted no time in scooping her up, he'd heard her mention her engagement to Dr. Monroe. "Thank you, ma'am. Thank you for saying such nice things about me."

"I have uttered the truth, Bray. The truth."

"Bray, this is Ms. Martha Purlasky and her daughter Megan. Cree and I performed an angioplasty on her not too long ago, and she is doing just fine, I'm happy to see."

"Waverly, please take Bray out onto the deck and enjoy the beauty of the afternoon. Megan will bring you out a cool drink shortly. Don't worry about lunch, my daughter is going to make you a seafood lasagna that you will never forget."

"Ms. Purlasky, I can't ask you…"

"It's okay, Mom. Let them make the lasagna for us. I love lasagna and appreciate their kindness in wanting to help you. You could use the rest, Mom."

Waverly still wasn't certain she should just turn her kitchen over to the Purlaskys, but she looked at them and realized they would be crushed if she didn't allow them to help. "Well, all right. I have made a salad already, it's in the fridge." She turned and placed her hands on Bray's wheelchair to wheel him out onto the deck, but before doing so, she turned and looked at Ms. Purlasky and Megan. "Thank you, thank you so much!"

Bray looked out over the lake; he was in deep thought, thinking about Dylan and how much he loved her. Thinking about how much he desperately wanted to marry her one day. But what kind of husband would he be? Things were different now. So much more different than they were the day he and Dylan had agreed they would get married after college. He loved her but how would he be able to make love to her? No, he was not going to hold her to the promise of marrying him no matter how much he loved her and she wanted it. She deserved better.

Dylan deserved a whole man, and Bray felt like only a half of one. He loved her too much not to give her his best and he would never be able to give her his best again, being dependent on a wheelchair.

"Bray?" The sound of Waverly's voice finally reached his ears and brought him back to the present.

"Sorry, Mom, I was just thinking about something."

"I know, I could tell. It's going to be all right, Bray. Everything is going to be okay. Your father and I don't want you to worry about a thing."

Megan walked out onto the deck carrying a tray of lemon iced tea and two tall glasses of ice. She sat the tray down on the coffee table and then took a damp cloth and wiped off the deck dining table before setting the tray and napkins on it. "Here you are, Mommy's special lemon iced tea. Enjoy it, I always do! It's delicious! Can I get you guys anything else?"

"No, Megan, thank you. You and your mother, it was so sweet of you to take the time out on such a beautiful afternoon to come over and spend time with Bray and me."

"Dr. Berman, this is just the beginning. Mommy and I, we will be coming by every Saturday to clean and cook a meal for you for the week. We have already discussed it. All we want you to be concerned about is taking care of Bray."

Waverly set her glass of tea down and cleared her throat. "Megan, I am so grateful that you and your mother want to help! Really, I am, but I'm afraid our family budget…"

LINDA MCCAIN

Waverly paused and looked down at the floor of the deck. "We don't have the finances to pay you and your mother."

"Pay us?" Megan said to Waverly as if she'd just spoken a foreign language.

"Yes, pay you for your services."

Megan smiled. "We are not looking for you to pay us. Mommy and I, we clean houses for a living and we get by just fine. We have about eight clients who all pay us very well plus tips. Now that Kerry and I are about to be married, Mommy and I have a little more financial freedom. Kerry has insisted that my mother come live with us after we are married. He said he doesn't want us to ever have to worry about paying rent or a bill again. He will take care of all of that." Megan stopped and thought before continuing, "But you know what, I'm not going to let him. I am still going to clean houses for earnings. I want to be a help to my husband. That's the way I was taught. The way my parents brought me up. To be a aide to your mate. So you see, there will be no need to pay us.

Your house, Dr. Berman, we are going to clean it for free and make wonderful meals for you and your family for the week. You and Dr. Hayes, you saved Mommy's life. Please don't tell her I shared this with you, but Dr. Hayes told us, she told us you put up over thirty percent of the money for Mommy's procedure and the medical care associated with it. Dr. Hayes put up over fifteen percent, and the rest was taken care of with financial assistance."

"Cree told you all of this, Megan?"

"Yes, but only after it slipped out. She and I were talking while at the hospital one day. When I showed her my engagement ring, she was so happy and excited! We just started talking about a lot of things, and it slipped out. I then asked her if she had also contributed a percentage to my mother's medical bills. I begged her to tell me, and finally she did."

Bray looked at Waverly; he knew his mother was a kind-hearted person but not to what extent until now. He loved his mother, and it pained him that she had to work so hard to help care for him. But he'd made up in his mind that after his first book became a bestseller, he would try to pay her back for at least some of the trouble he'd put her through.

"Here it is now, just look at that apple pie. Is that not the prettiest golden-brown crust you've ever seen?" Ms. Purlasky said as she joined them on the deck. They all agreed that it was. "Megan, check on your lasagna. Bray looks hungry, I'll bring out the plates and utensils. Waverly, would you please give me a hand in the kitchen?"

"Sure, of course!" Waverly followed Ms. Purlasky into the kitchen. She stopped just inside the door. She couldn't believe it. All the clutter that had accumulated was gone, the hardwood floors sparkled, and everything on the counter tops were neat and orderly.

"Ms. Purlasky, thank you so much! I hardly recognize this as being my kitchen. You and Megan are miracle workers!"

"I was always taught, Dr. Berman, that you don't have to have the best for it to look the best. Just keep whatever it is neat and clean and you will have the best of it. Ms. Purlasky wiped her hands on her apron nervously and cleared her throat before saying, "Dr. Berman, I don't mean to pry into your personal affairs, but Bray, he is a good one.

I know he is. I can see it in his eyes. He wants nothing but good for others. Yet he has been dealt a lousy hand. He is trying to make the best of it, but something is hurting him deeply. Something besides being in that wheelchair."

Waverly picked up the dishcloth and wiped off the kitchen table, although it was spotless, thanks to Megan and Ms. Purlasky. "My son, he was supposed to marry his high school sweetheart after college. Now he feels he has nothing to offer her, so he has decided not to marry her."

"The lasagna is ready. Should I take it out to the deck now?"

"Not right now, Megan. I want you to stay here and talk with Dr. Berman for a little while. Bring everything out to the deck in about twenty minutes."

"Okay." Megan and Waverly looked at Ms. Purlasky, who looked hurt but said nothing.

Bray looked up at her as Ms. Purlasky came out the door. "Hi!"

"Hi, son. It's a beautiful day, isn't it?"

"Yes ma'am, it sure is."

"You know, Bray, when my husband was alive, on days like this, he and I would take a long ride on the back roads where we lived. Then we would stop at a nearby diner for a bite to eat. My husband was so kind, never a hurtful word would he speak to me. Oh, we had our disagreements just like most couples do, but our words were never harsh and biting. And you know why?" Bray thought for a second, trying more so to figure out why Ms. Purlasky was telling him these things.

"Why?"

"Because when you love someone, truly love someone, you want them to be happy and you will do all within your power to make sure it's so for them."

"Yes ma'am."

"The best show of love my husband ever gave me came from his simple acts of kindness toward me, not his genitalia, if you understand what I mean?" Bray looked at Ms. Purlasky and smiled.

"Yes, ma'am, I know exactly what you mean."

When Ms. Purlasky and Megan washed up the last dish, tidied up the kitchen, and packed their bags to leave, Bray began to feel sad. He'd enjoyed having them spend the afternoon with them. "Ms. Purlasky, the lasagna was great. Can't wait to try it again sometime."

"Oh, don't you worry, Bray, you will be trying a lot of our food. Just you wait and see." Megan picked up her bags and then helped her mom with hers. "We will see you at the end of the week, Dr. Berman. Let's go now, Megan, so they can get some rest."

Chapter 14

Noel and TJ had decided it best to discontinue the Monday Night Chat Sessions for a while. At least until Bray was strong enough to travel from house to house for the sessions. None of them felt very chatty, anyway; they were all still trying to adjust to Bray being in a wheelchair. Jermaine was more upset than anyone, even Dylan, it seemed. There were days when he was so angry and so hurt all he could do was go on a basketball court and shoot a few hoops until sweat covered his body. Sometimes he would leave early in the morning, well before his dad was up, just so he wouldn't have to talk to or see anyone. But this morning, he waited for his dad to come downstairs. He wanted to see him, talk to him. He wanted to know why it was taking so long to find the person who hit Bray.

Jermaine sat on the bottom step leading from the upstairs bedrooms in his house. When he heard his father's bedroom door open, he called to him. "Dad! Dad, are you up?" Robbie rolled his eyes and sighed heavily. He was not in the mood this morning to answer Jermaine's questions about the investigation of Bray's car accident. He had nothing, absolutely nothing to tell him. No witnesses, no wreckage pieces from the accident other than what came from Waverly's car, which wasn't much since it was basically totaled in the car accident. All he really had were pictures of Waverly's car taken after the accident.

"Good morning, J," Robbie said as he ran down the steps, heading for the front door.

"Dad, you got a minute, please?"

"J, I got to get to work. Can this wait until this evening?"

"I know, I know," Jermaine rushed to say. "But, Dad, I don't understand why you guys haven't found anything yet. It's going on two months now and not a word regarding Bray's accident, nothing!"

"J, it's not that easy. This type of investigation takes time."

"I want to help you. I want to help you look for the person who hit Bray that night on Lombar Road. Just tell me what you need me to do and I'm on it!" Robbie looked at his son.

"Jermaine, the best thing you can do right now to help Bray is to just be there for him. Be his friend."

"I am his friend, Dad, his best friend. That's why I want to help find the person who put him in that wheelchair. I just want to know how they feel. I want to know if whoever it was, knows what it's like to watch someone you love suffer in silence as a result of some reckless driver's carelessness. I bet the person was drunk! No! I can't just sit back and wait for the cops to play the guessing game. I want to know who put Bray in that chair, and if you can't give me answers, then I will just have to search for them on my own! Have a good day, Dad!" Jermaine opened the door and walked out, slamming it behind him.

*****

169

As Nevin drove home from work that evening, he reflected on his night out with Bray. It was good, very good. They both enjoyed the movie and a quick stop at an ice cream shop for a sundae on the way home. He felt like he was connecting with Bray—something he wished he'd done long before the accident.

Bray had complimented him on his new car, said it was awesome! Nevin had never considered buying a Mercedes before. However, he felt now was as good a time as any, plus he needed something to boost his spirits. When he traded his old car in, the dealer asked about his license plates because there was only one. The only thing he could think of was that the other one must have come off when he hit the deer on Lombar Road that night, so he had to get new ones.

After learning of Bray's car accident, Nevin's spirits sank to an all-time low. Drinking didn't even help; the more he drank, the worse he felt. Nothing seemed to dull the pain he was experiencing. Buying the Mercedes only served as a Band-Aid that covered a permanent deep gash in his heart—a gash that was too deep to ever heal. He'd wanted to drive off a cliff and end it all, thinking that there was no way possible a person could feel the way he did and endure life every day. He then realized how selfish and cowardly the act would be. Waverly, Ellis, Noi, and, more importantly, Bray needed him now more than ever.

As Nevin turned down Lombar Road headed home, he noticed Jermaine's jeep parked by the side of the road. Jermaine emerged out of the woods that lined the road. Nevin slowed down and pulled up beside him. "Hey, Jermaine, what's going on? You all right, son?"

"Hey, Mr. Berman, yeah, I'm fine. I just thought I would look around, looking for something, anything that will give me a clue as to what happened that night on this road, the night of Bray's car accident."

Nevin pulled over, parked his car then got out and walked slowly over to Jermaine. He was tired, he'd had a rough day, and all he really wanted to do was get home. "I know what you mean, son. I came down this road headed home the same night of Bray's accident. It's funny, at the time, there was no indication that there had been an accident. I don't know, I keep trying to revisit that night, but it's somewhat of a blur. I just don't know, I hit a deer that night, I must have because something tore the front bumper off my car."

"Man, Mr. Berman, I hope you weren't hurt. Did you get out to see if it was actually a deer you hit?"

"No, I just assumed, had to be a deer, what else could it have been?" Jermaine stared at him but said nothing.

"Didn't hurt myself though, not too badly. I hit my head pretty bad, though, had to have a few stitches."

"I'm really sorry to hear that."

"Well, I'd better get on in. Waverly has been with Bray all day. I need to get home to start my shift of caring for him. Good to see you, Jermaine. Don't stay out too long, son. It's getting late and this road is dark, no streetlights. It's a wonder there hasn't been more car accidents on this road."

"Yes, sir, I will be leaving soon. Just want to look around a little more."

Nevin said good night to Jermaine, got in his car, and drove off. Jermaine waved at him and then turned around to search Lombar Road a little more while the light lasted. It was dusk and Jermaine thought to himself, Lombar Road was the last place he wanted to be at night. He started walking up and down the side of the road, keeping his eyes glued to the ground. That's when he saw it, the license plate. He looked at it and then went to pick it up. His cell phone rang in that same instant, causing him to turn his attention away from the license plate. "Hello."

"Hey, J! What's up? I haven't heard from you all day. I sent you a few text messages but nothing. You okay?"

"Hey, Bray, I'm fine, man. I'm out and about, was going to stop by on my way home. You need anything?"

"Nope, just wanted to know what you were up to. Why don't you head on over now? Mom just made your favorite, burgers and fries!"

"Say what? I'm on my way!" Jermaine hung up his call with Bray, put his cell phone back in his pocket, and then jogged back to his truck and pulled off.

Noel opened the door for Jermaine and stepped aside for him to walk in. She tried to take a quick glance at him as he walked past her, but he stopped and pulled off his jacket, causing her to turn away quickly so he wouldn't catch her trying to check him out. "Dang, I wish I was older. Whoever gets J is going to be one lucky woman," she said low enough for Jermaine not to hear her.

"What's up, Noi? Where should I put my jacket?"

"Here, I'll take it. Nice jacket, J. Is it new?"

"Nah, I just don't wear it that often. It was a gift from an old girlfriend, so I kind of keep it hidden in the back of my closet. Just grabbed it today because it was the lightest thing I could find." Noel smiled.

"Old girlfriend, J? So what's your new girlfriend up to? You should bring her around sometime so we can meet her." Jermaine laughed and shoved Noel playfully.

"No new girlfriend, Noi. I'm looking but not too hard. I'm enjoying being a single man. No hassles! I am going to head on back to see Bray."

"Okay."

Bray looked up from his computer as Jermaine walked in. "Thanks for inviting me over for dinner."

"You know this is just as much your home as it is mine, Jermaine. What's going on? Unlike you not to check in."

"I'm cool. I been playing cop since my dad and his partner can't seem to get it right, trying to help them out."

"Cop, what do you mean?"

Jermaine picked Bray's basketball up off the floor and started tossing it in the air. "I know you are not going to like what I'm about to say, Bray, but I'm going to say it, anyway. I went over to Lombar Road today, searching for something that would point us in the right direction."

"Right direction?"

"I want to know who hit you, Bray. I'm looking for *anything* that will put me on the trail of the person who hit you head-on that night on Lombar Road."

Bray turned and looked at the wall behind his bed. "J…"

"Who hit you, Bray? Man, why do I feel like you know more than what you're saying? Why is it that every time I try to talk to you about that night, you shut me down?"

"Why can't you let it go, J! What's done is done! Finding the person who hit me is not going to undo what has been done. This is it, J, this is my life now. I've accepted it, so why can't you?"

Jermaine let out a deep breath and looked out the window to calm himself. "You know what, Bray, let's just drop it for now because I'm getting mad and I don't want to do that! I refuse to let the person who put you in that chair cause an argument between you and me. Let's just go enjoy your mom's burgers." Jermaine threw the basketball against the wall and stormed out of Bray's room. Bray shook his head and wheeled his chair out behind him.

Chapter 15

Jessica pulled off her sunglasses and looked around the hospital grounds. The sun beat down on her, causing her to feel annoyed and hot. She took her time walking toward the hospital entrance, scolding herself all the while for deciding to wear heels instead of a reasonable pair of walking shoes. *Well, I am not a reasonable kind of woman, so there, thus the heels. Plus, reasonable shoes would destroy my three-thousand-dollar outfit.* After stopping and pulling out her cell phone, she dialed Cree's number and prayed to God she'd answer before her makeup melted off her face.

"Hey, Jess, are you here?" Cree answered.

"Yep, where are you? Should I come up?"

"Nope, I'm heading down. Waverly is waiting in the lobby already."

"Okay, I'm going to get back in my car. I will just meet you guys at the restaurant."

"Okay, Waverly is riding with me, so we will be there shortly. You know where we are going, right?"

"Dad's restaurant, right?"

"Yes, ma'am. See you soon!"

By the time Cree and Waverly reached the restaurant, Jessica was already seated. She spotted them as they walked in and waved them over. "Hi, Waverly!" Jessica said a little too cheerfully as Cree and Waverly approached her. *Too much, Jess, bring it down a notch*, Cree thought. Waverly laughed.

"Hi, Jessica, good to see you. You doing all right?"

"Yep, with Doc Hayes on my back, I have no choice. Good to see you, Waverly. I've ordered a glass of wine for us and a couple of appetizers."

Cree glanced at Waverly. "I'm glad you decided to join us for lunch today, Waverly. Get out, get some sunshine. When I talked to Ms. Purlasky and asked her if she would be willing to sit with Bray a little while today so you could have lunch with us, she was so happy!"

"Ms. Purlasky, what a sweetheart," Waverly said softly.

"She truly is. She stopped by the hospital yesterday to drop me off yet another pumpkin pie. So help me, if that Martha Purlasky brings me one more pumpkin pie, I don't know what I am going to do. I have already put on about five pounds as a result of those pies!" Waverly looked down.

"Thank you, Cree."

"Sure!"

"I guess I've forgotten what it's like to have the freedom to just get out. I've gotten so used to staying in with Bray and caring for him. I don't know how to act, really. I mean, I'm not complaining about it. It's just nice to be out is what I'm trying to say."

"Hey, why don't we go all out? This is a special occasion! It's on the house, whatever you want, just go for it," Jessica said cheerfully.

Cree and Waverly laughed and then picked up their menu. When Waverly started to cry, Cree looked at her, and Jessica got up and ran to the bathroom for tissue. "I'm sorry, I'm so sorry. I told myself I wouldn't do this. I just... Cree, how did this happen? This was not supposed to happen! Bray should be planning to leave for Northwestern University in the fall!"

Jessica returned with the tissues and handed them to Waverly. "Listen, I think we are going to need a designated driver. We need something a little stronger than wine. Cree, I will leave my car here at the restaurant, and you drive home so Waverly and I can get drunk!" They all burst into uncontrollable laughter, and Jessica motioned for a waiter to come over as they were ready to order.

"Everything looks so good on this menu, but I'm not really hungry." Jessica took the menu from Waverly and looked through it.

"I'll pick something out for you. You're hungry, you've just forgotten what hunger feels like. I bet you make sure Bray has three good meals every day, but you, you hardly ever eat, am I right?" Jessica asked.

"Well, I guess you are."

"Waverly, you have lost some weight," Cree said with concern.

"Here we go!" Jessica said excitedly. "This is perfect, tasty, and filling. I will order for you, Waverly! Cree, if you're ready to order, I know what I want also."

"Yep, ready." When the waiter returned to their table with a basket of bread, Jessica ordered coq au vin for Waverly and duck confit for herself. Cree also went with the duck confit. "Gabriel, please bring us another bottle of wine," Jessica said. Cree wondered how Jessica knew the waiter's name and then remembered they were having lunch at one of Jessica's father's French restaurants.

"Hey, guys, guess what?"

"What?" Jessica said as she took a sip of her wine.

"Megan and Dr. Kerry Monroe are engaged."

"What! Since when?"

"Cree, you mean to tell me with all the pumpkin pies Ms. Purlasky has been bringing you, she never once mentioned her daughter's engagement to Kerry?"

"No, never! Oh, wait! I forgot! Megan did mention her engagement and showed me her amazing ring!"

"Who is Megan?" Jessica wanted to know.

Cree turned to Jessica. "Megan is the daughter of one of our patients. Rumor has it that she and one of our surgeons, Kerry Monroe, met while she was waiting for her mother. Her mother was having a procedure performed at the hospital the day they met. Megan is absolutely gorgeous inside and out!"

"Well, so am I, Cree, but you don't see any doctors banging down my door. Sounds like I need to visit you more at Simon Memorial," Jessica said with a smile.

Cree laughed. "Jess, your day will come. It will, in time."

"I sure hope so, Cree!"

"What about you, ma'am? Is there an interest?"

"Jess, you know me, I can be difficult when it comes to men. I'm very selective, and rightfully so. After Dylan's father left me to care for her on my own, I don't take dating too lightly."

Waverly cleared her throat and looked at Cree out of the corner of her eye. "Jess, Cree had this handsome doctor after her. I mean the man is fine and loaded!" Jessica looked at Cree as if she was mental.

"Look, if you don't want him, give me his number."

"It's not that simple, Jess."

"Yes, it is. Give me his number and I will show you just how simple it is."

"Girl, you are crazy," Cree said to Jessica as she picked up her glass of water to drink.

"So are you going to let something like that get away?"

The waiter walked up with their food and set their individual dishes in front of them and then popped open a bottle of champagne. "Champagne! I think it goes to another table, sir."

"Oh, he is at the right table, Cree. I sent him a text to bring it out with our meals. I know the cell numbers of all the staff here as well as their names. Dad put me in charge of this particular restaurant." Jessica looked at Cree, "So?"

"So, what?"

"Are you going to pursue this interest or not?"

"Not! Dating is over for me. Dylan's dad destroyed it for me, but it's nice to have friends…safer this way, no risk of getting hurt again." Jessica and Waverly looked at her sadly before Jessica said, "One day you and I are going to revisit this conversation Cree."

"It must be nice to be in charge of this restaurant for your dad," Waverly said to Jessica.

"It is," Jessica responded with a smile.

Waverly was picking at her food; her mind kept wandering to Bray. She wondered what he was doing, how he was doing, and if Ms. Purlasky was doing okay helping him

179

with everything he needed. "Waverly, stop stressing. Eat, enjoy this wonderful food."

"I'm sorry, Jessica, you're right, this food is so delicious, but…" Waverly looked at each of them. "I hate to ruin our lunch with my woes."

"Waverly, talk to us. We are here for you. You know that."

"Thank you, Jessica."

"Well, ever since the accident, even with our savings, the medical bills have been escalating. The insurance is helping, but with Bray's meds being so expensive, I'm concerned that what we need the most for him we won't be able to afford."

"Yeah, and what do you need for him?"

"Cree, we really need a full-time nurse for Bray, at least until he gets his strength back."

Jessica continued to eat and pretended to ignore the conversation. Waverly looked at her. "I'm sorry, Jess."

"Sorry for what? You have something that's bothering you and you need to voice it. There is no harm in that. You know, Waverly, I would love to meet Bray. Why don't you give me your address? Perhaps I can stop by tomorrow. Okay with you?"

"Sure, of course, he loves having visitors."

"Great, I will be there around two."

After they finished their lunch, they sat and talked for a bit longer before Cree said she had to get back to the hospital. Waverly said she had to get back to Bray and Jess had a nail appointment. Jessica offered to take Waverly home, but she thanked her and declined, then ordered an uber.

Cree smiled and said, "See you later guys, I really need to get back to the hospital now."

"Oh, Waverly, your address?"

"Sure, sorry." Waverly wrote down her address and handed it to Jessica, and then they left the restaurant.

Waverly walked in the door to her house, and the aroma of baking bread greeted her. She walked in the kitchen, and there sat Bray with a plate full of food in front of him. Ms. Purlasky was at the stove cooking even more food.

"Bray, honey, are you going to be able to eat all of that?"

"No. I tried to tell her that, but…"

"You are a growing boy. You must eat. Eat to keep that glowing skin and beautiful hair. You look like a skeleton sitting in that chair. Oh, but that's about to change. Now eat!"

Waverly laughed. "Ms. Purlasky…?"

"It's okay, Mom, I'm fine. This baked fish is the best, and I don't even like fish." Waverly smiled at her son and then walked over and hugged him.

"Enjoy yourself, son."

"Now you go rest. I will bring a plate in to you."

"Oh my gosh, thank you, but I just ate lunch, Ms. Purlasky."

"Then I'll wrap it up for your dinner. Go rest now. I have nothing better to do this afternoon, plus Bray and I are having ourselves a fine time, aren't we, Bray?"

"Yes, ma'am, we sure are. Go rest, Mom."

Dylan walked in the back door leading to the Berman kitchen and gently closed it behind her. Bray's back was turned to her. Dylan looked at Ms. Purlasky, puzzled. "Who are you?"

"That's a question I should be asking you, walking up in this house without knocking first."

"It's okay, Ms. Purlasky," Bray said while turning around to look at Dylan. "This is Dylan, a friend of mine." Walking over to the table and setting the basket of fruit down she'd bought for Bray, Dylan looked at him.

"*Friend?* Is that what I am to you now, Bray?" Dylan was hurt and didn't try to conceal it. Bray turned back around to finish his plate without responding to Dylan.

Ms. Purlasky looked at Bray, waiting for him to respond to Dylan without her having to encourage him to. But Bray said nothing. "I am going to check on your mother, Bray, see if she needs anything. In the meantime, try to shake loose that cat that's got your tongue and be the polite young man I know you are. Dylan asked you a question." Ms. Purlasky picked up the dish towel and wiped her hands on it and then walked quietly out of the kitchen, leaving Bray and Dylan alone to talk.

"How are you feeling today, Bray?" Dylan paused before continuing, "I took my braids out, did my hair. Do you like it? I think you prefer it this way. The curls are still a little tight, but they will fall to just the way you like it." Bray looked up from his plate at Dylan.

"Nice, your hair looks nice, Dylan." Dylan quickly picked up the basket of fruit and took out an apple.

"I brought you some apples, I know how much you like apples. I could peel one for you right now if you'd like." Bray slowly shook his head no, in response to Dylan, then turned and looked out the window.

"Dylan...this is not going to work."

"Bray, please?"

MY FATHER, MY SON

"Look at me, I'm in a wheelchair, Dylan. What is wrong with you? Why do you still want to be with me?"

Dylan looked at him for a second before saying, "Because I love you, Bray, that's why."

The door opened, and Bray and Dylan turned to see Ellis walking in the door. Ellis stopped in his tracks. "Man, what's up? You both look like you've seen a ghost." Ellis waited for Bray and Dylan to respond to what he'd just said, but neither of them did. Ellis then shook his head and walked past them to his room.

*****

Waverly stared down at the envelope in her hand addressed to her and tried to figure out who could have possibly left it for her. It had been a strange day, she thought. First, she'd had trouble getting Bray to eat his breakfast. She finally gave up on that and decided to wait for lunchtime. She figured he'd be starving by then. He had to be because he hadn't eaten or drunk anything all day. She was worried and made up her mind to call his doctor in the morning if he didn't get better. He had to be sick, she knew her son, he loved food.

In addition to not being able to get Bray to eat, Jessica called to say she would not be able to make it over to see Bray today as planned because something had come up at her dad's restaurant and they needed her there. She apologized profusely and said she would call to set up another time to visit with Bray.

Now this envelope addressed to her with $50,000 in cash inside. There was no return address. Just a typed note

183

saying, "Waverly, I heard about your son's car accident. I hope this cash will be of some help to you." There wasn't even a signature. Whoever left it, slid it under the door, which Waverly found to be very odd, she couldn't understand why the person didn't at least leave their name or knock on the door and give it directly to her.

Chapter 16

Nevin sat at his desk staring down at a blank sheet of paper. He'd been sitting there like that for close to an hour, trying to compose a letter of agreement. He felt nervous and anxious, the result of not taking a drink in over two weeks, not one. He wanted to drink so badly, dull the ache in his heart over Bray. Every time he poured a glass of wine, liquor, or any alcohol, period, visions of Bray's body in a wheelchair came to mind. Robbie's words came to him every time he even started to drink. *"I'm convinced that whoever hit Bray that night was drunk."*

Try as he might to remember that night on Lombar Road, the night of Bray's car accident, he couldn't. He remembered taking Lombar Road home that same night, but there was nothing, not one sign of an accident. Nevin shook his head and picked up the sheet of paper only to ball it up and toss it in the trash. "Why, why can't I remember what happened that night? I remember being drunk and trying to make it home and then hitting something… It had to be a deer, what else could it have been?" he said to himself.

His desk phone rang, and he looked at it, annoyed, because he didn't feel like talking to anyone. But he answered anyway because someone was calling him from home. "Yeah!"

"Hey, Dad, how is it going? What time do you think you will be in tonight? Mom is making baked salmon, your favorite," Bray said cheerfully.

"I'm not sure, son. I still have a lot of work to finish up here. How are you feeling?"

"I'm great, Dad, just fine. Listen, I won't keep you. Get back to work so hopefully you will make it home in time to eat dinner with us, okay?"

"Okay, son, sure. I will do my best."

"Great, see you soon."

Waverly walked into Bray's room just as he ended the call with Nevin. She smiled at him and then walked over and hugged him tightly. "What was that for, Mom?"

"Just because." Bray smiled at his mother and wheeled his chair over to the window and looked out at the lake.

"The lake, it's beautiful, Mom. I'm glad you chose this house."

"Yes, it is, isn't it? Would you like me to wheel you outside so you can enjoy the evening? The sun is setting, it's beautiful out there."

"No thanks, Mom, but thank you, anyway."

"Bray, Officer McBride is in the living room. He asked me to see if you felt up to answering a few questions about…about the night of your accident. He said it won't take long. I thought if I wheeled you onto the deck, the two of you could talk there. It would be a more relaxed atmosphere."

"So that's why you offered to wheel me outside, so I could talk to him?"

"No, son, I just thought it would be nice for you to get some fresh air while speaking with him if you chose to do so."

"Mom, would you please tell Officer McBride that I'm not up to talking about the accident right now?"

Waverly shook her head and tried to clear her mind. "Bray, please talk to Robbie. You must remember something about that night, the night of the accident!" Bray was angry; he wheeled his chair around too fast to face Waverly and he fell out of it. Waverly ran to him. "Oh my god, Bray! Oh my god, son! Are you all right?" Waverly was trying to get him up off the floor, but Bray pushed her away.

"Leave me alone, just leave me alone," he yelled at her. "Why does everyone keep asking me the same questions repeatedly! I told all of you all I can! When his car headed straight at me..." Bray stopped talking suddenly, realizing what he'd just said. "I mean, when the car came straight at me, I didn't know what to do! I panicked! I panicked! Had I remained calm, the driver may never have hit me. It wasn't his fault! It was my fault, all my fault! He didn't mean to hit me! He didn't!"

Waverly looked at Bray and then turned to see Officer McBride standing in the doorway. He'd come running to Bray's room when he heard the crash of Bray's fall. Robbie walked slowly over to Bray, his mind lingering on what he'd just heard Bray say, *he*. Robbie reached down, picked Bray up off the floor, and helped him back in the wheelchair. He stood and looked at Bray for a second. "Who hit you that night, Bray, on Lombar Road?" Bray didn't answer him.

Waverly was still on the floor from where she'd tried to help Bray get back in his chair. She looked up at him. "Son, do you know who hit you? You said *he*, Bray. Did you see the person who hit you head-on that night?" Bray turned away from Robbie and Waverly.

"Will you two please leave my room? I'd like to be left alone."

Waverly rubbed her hands on her jeans and got up off the floor. She looked at Robbie and slowly shook her head. "Come on, Waverly, let's leave Bray to rest for now."

"Son, are you all right?"

Silence hung in the air before Bray responded, "Yes, Mom, I'm fine."

Robbie walked out of Bray's room, and Waverly followed. She was sad and confused. She wanted to know why Bray said *he* when he referred to the person who hit him the night of his accident. She looked at Robbie as he stood in the middle of her living room floor, deep in thought over the information Bray had just revealed. Her eyes begged Robbie for answers.

Robbie looked at her and rubbed the back of his head and then said softly to Waverly, "Bray knows who hit him that night. Question is, why is he not saying? Has he been threatened by someone not to say anything?"

"No, Robbie! No! If he knew, if Bray knew who hit him, he would tell us! He wouldn't keep something like that from you, from me!" Waverly said while pointing to herself. Robbie walked slowly to the door, opened it, and walked out without saying another word.

"Mom." Waverly turned to see Bray in the room looking at her. He was hurt, she could tell; the emotion filled his eyes.

"Yes, Bray, what is it, son?"

"I'm sorry, I'm sorry I yelled. I'm sorry I wouldn't let you help me off the floor. It's just that…I need to learn to help myself. I may have to be on my own one day, without the help of my family. I don't want to be dependent on other people for help. I just want to be able to do things for myself, that's all." Waverly couldn't say anything; she just looked at her son, her heart breaking. Finally, she nodded her head that she understood.

*****

Dylan looked at her reflection in the floor-length mirror in her room and then touched the curls in her hair as she bit on her bottom lip and tried to squash the depression associated with she and Bray's dwindling relationship. "What's wrong with me? Why don't you want me, Bray?" she said to herself. Cree knocked softly on her door.

"Hey, you, Aunt Jess is here. Why don't you come out and say hello to her? She brought food, French food, the best!"

"Sure, Mom, just give me a minute. I'll be right there."

"Okay, we will be in the kitchen!"

Dylan turned away from the mirror, pinched her cheeks to give them some color, and walked to the kitchen. "Hey, Aunt Jess!"

"Hey, Dylan, I love your hair! It's awesome!"

"Thank you, Aunt Jess." Cree looked at Dylan and then cut her eye at Jessica. Something was on Dylan's mind, she could tell. She'd learned a long time ago the importance of being able to read Dylan's actions, not to just understand what she chose to tell her, and right now, Dylan's body language was screaming *"Help me!"*

Jessica noticed something was wrong, too, so she got up and walked over to Dylan. "Your mom won't ask, but I will. What's up?"

"Nothing, Aunt Jess, I'm good and I'm hungry. I'm going to go wash up for dinner. I'll be right back!"

Jessica turned and looked at Cree. "What's going on, Cree? What's wrong with her? Do you know?"

"I think I do but I will have to discuss it with you later."

"I don't want to discuss it later. I want to know now! I want to know who or what has Dylan so upset!"

"Jess, hush! She will hear you!"

"Good! I don't care! I just want to know what's bothering her. Maybe she will tell me if she hears me talking about her."

Dylan came back in the room and sat at the table, she looked down at her hands and started playing with her fingers nervously. "Mom, Aunt Jess, do you think I'm pretty?" Jessica and Cree looked at each other.

"Yes, you are, you are very pretty, Dylan. Why do you ask that question? Did someone say something about the way you look?" Jessica said angrily.

"No, not at all. I was just wondering. Can we eat now? I'm really hungry."

"Well, not me! I just lost my appetite! I want to know who said something to you, Dylan!"

"Jess, it's okay. Let's just leave it for now. I'm sure Dylan will confide in us when she is ready. But for now, let's just enjoy this delicious dinner you brought us." Cree turned and started taking down plates and then pulling out silverware while thinking to herself, *Don't you worry, Jessica. I will get to the bottom of it, and it will be tonight.*

There was a slight breeze coming through Dylan's window as she lay in bed that night. Her thoughts wandered to Bray and the fact that in a few months, she would be leaving for medical school. She felt an overwhelming sadness and a fear of the unknown. Turning to her journal and pulling up the covers under her chin was her way of relaxing so she could drift off to sleep. She slid down further in her bed and opened her journal, dated it, and then wrote down her thoughts.

> *I used to think that when you were young, nothing bad could happen to you. A few weeks ago, Bray and I were shopping for our prom, a prom we never made it to. Bray is paralyzed now from the waist down, and I am paralyzed with fear that things will never be the same between us. I wish I knew what to say to him, what to do, to let him know that he being paralyzed doesn't change the way I feel about him. But...*

Dylan stopped writing and looked at her door as Cree walked in.

"Hi, Mom!"

"Hey, what are you doing?" Dylan looked down at her journal and then slowly closed it; she didn't want her mother to see what she'd written.

"Nothing much, just writing in my journal." Cree gently pulled the journal out of Dylan's hands and laid it on her nightstand.

"Dylan, I need to ask you something." Dylan looked at Cree and tried to figure out what was going on; she looked so serious.

"What is it, Mom? Is something wrong? Have I done something wrong?"

"No, honey, you haven't done a thing wrong."

Cree looked down at Dylan's bedspread, searching for the right words, the right way to ask her about her relationship with Bray. But the more she thought about it, there were no right words she could think of, and being a mother of a seventeen-year-old doesn't come with an instruction manual. You just have to feel your way and hope for the best, she thought.

"Dylan, is everything okay with you and Bray?"

"What do you mean?"

"Well, I haven't heard you say much about him lately, so I was just wondering, you know, if you were still seeing each other?" Dylan didn't answer right away; instead, she looked out the window, in the direction of Bray's house.

"Bray and I are not seeing each other right now. I guess you could say we are taking a break."

"When…when did you guys decide to take a break from each other?" Dylan shrugged her shoulders.

"I don't know, really. I guess he figures that now that he is confined to a wheelchair for the most part, he has nothing to offer me. I've tried to tell him that's not true, but he refuses to listen."

"Dylan, I want you to get some sleep now, it's late. I'm very sorry to hear that things have kind of cooled off between you and Bray. Before I leave this room, I need to know how you feel about it, if you are okay."

"Sure, Mom, I'm fine with it. The way Bray is feeling about us right now is only temporary, I know it is. So I will just have to wait, wait until he realizes he is making a mistake, that he has a lot to offer me and I have a lot to offer him. We are going to be fine."

"Okay, just so you are all right. If you ever feel the need to talk to me more about this, you know I'm here for you no matter what time of the day or night it is, right?" Dylan nodded her head that she understood.

"Good night, Mom, I'm tired now. I will see you in the morning."

"Good night, Dylan." Cree walked to Dylan's door, and before turning off the light, she looked back at her and then walked out of the room, closing the door gently behind her.

*****

Robbie McBride sat at his kitchen table and nursed a glass of water while glancing at the front door, hoping Jermaine would walk through it at any moment, and when he did, Robbie breathed a sigh of relief. Ever since Bray's car accident, he kept in the back of his mind that what happened to Bray on Lombar Road could have happened to anyone, even his son.

"Hey, Dad, it's late. Why are you still up?"

"I was just sitting here waiting for you to come in. I need to talk to you about something. Where have you been, son?" Jermaine walked to the hall closet and hung up his jacket and then exhaled.

"I drove over to Lombar Road. I just kept turning off it and getting back on that road, driving down it, looking for something, anything that would give a clue as to what happened on that road the night of Bray's accident."

"Jermaine, you have got to leave it up to us to find out what happened that night."

"Dad, I'm trying to, but it just seems like it's taking you guys so long to come up with anything! At least something! It's been a while now and still nothing! This is a small town. It just shouldn't be this hard to find out who hit Bray that night."

"Jermaine, I think Bray may know who hit him that night."

"What?"

"I said, I think he knows. He knows who hit him, but for some reason, he won't say."

"You know, Dad, I kind of get the same feeling. I don't know what it is, but every time I try to talk to him about that night, he gets tired or wants to change the subject. Something is wrong with that. I just wish I could get him to open up to me, talk to me, tell me something…give me some hope that one day we are going to catch the lowlife that put him in that chair."

"I know how you feel, Jermaine. Like you, I want nothing more than to catch the person who hit Bray that night."

"Dad, there is something else I need to discuss with you." Robbie looked at Jermaine and waited for him to continue. "I've decided not to go to Harvard. I'm staying here and going to Virginia School of Law."

"Jermaine…"

"Dad, please, just hear me out. If I'm going to become a lawyer, I'm going to become a lawyer regardless of where I go to college. The name of the school you attended is just an eye-opener when it comes to applying to firms for a position. My grades and passing the bar will be the *door opener*. I was a straight A student in high school, Dad. I'm determined to be a straight A student in college." Jermaine paused and walked toward the stairs leading to the bedrooms. "I'm going to be a lawyer and a good one! But foremost, I'm going to be here for Bray. I appreciate all the hard work and overtime you've put in just so I could have a choice in law schools to attend. I love you, Dad. Trust, I'm not going to disappoint you. Good night."

Robbie watched Jermaine walk out of the room and said nothing; he knew it wouldn't do any good. His son's mind was made up. "I know you are not going to disappointment me, Jermaine, you never have," Robbie said to himself and then turned off the light and went upstairs to bed.

Chapter 17

Martha Purlasky dropped her bags at the Berman door and then turned around to see what was keeping Megan. "Megan! Come quickly, what's keeping you? I may be the sickly one, but heaven knows you're the slow one. A turtle would have made it to this door by now!"

"Mommy, you gave me a million bags to carry!"

"Well, I carried a million and one, so what does that tell you?" Megan just shook her head and mumbled under her breath as she continued to struggle to get the bags to the door.

When Ms. Purlasky knocked on the door, Noel opened it. A bowl of cereal was in her hand, her hair piled on top of her head. "Ms. Purlasky, what are you doing here? It's nine thirty on a Saturday morning."

"I know what day it is, Noi, and guess what, I can tell time too. Here is a bit of encouraging information for you to think about, my dear. When you get to be my age, you will still be able to keep up with the days of the week and tell time. How about that, isn't that good news?" Noel smiled and stepped aside to let Ms. Purlasky in. She looked up and saw Megan struggling with bags. She set her bowl of cereal down and ran out to help her.

When Ellis saw Ms. Purlasky walk in the door, he yelled upstairs to Waverly, "Mom, that lady is here!" Ms. Purlasky walked over to Ellis and smiled at him.

"Let me ask you something, son, how old are you?" Ellis looked at Ms. Purlasky uncertainly, not knowing why she'd just questioned him.

"I'm sixteen."

"Well, from this day forward, I want you to remember something. Every time you see me walk through that front door, you remember this, my name is Ms. Purlasky. Oh yes, I am a lady, but my name is Ms. Purlasky. You remember that, okay?" Ellis looked at Ms. Purlasky for a second and then at Megan as she and Noel walked in carrying their bags.

"Yes, ma'am, I'll remember. Is that your daughter?"

"Yes, it is. You also remember this. My daughter is twenty-five and engaged." With that, Ms. Purlasky walked to the kitchen while motioning for Megan to follow her.

When Waverly finally made it downstairs and walked in the kitchen, she was greeted with the smell of bacon, and her kitchen looked like it belonged to someone else. She could see from one side of the room to the other without the obstruction of clutter. "Ms. Purlasky, Megan, good morning. I didn't expect you so early. I just finished helping Bray with his bath. What can I do to help?"

"Nothing, you sit down. I'll make you a cup of coffee."

"Okay, thank you, I appreciate that."

Waverly tried to tuck a few stray strands of her hair back in place and then walked over and sat down opposite Megan, who was pulling out containers of food from the bags. Waverly glanced at Megan. "Hey, Megan, how are you feeling this morning? How are the wedding plans coming along?" Waverly said with a smile.

"Hey, Dr. Berman. I'm great and my wedding plans are coming along nicely. It's not going to be a very large wedding. Mommy and I don't have the money for that, but it's going to be a beautiful one! I've always wanted an outdoor evening wedding if ever I got married."

"Oh, Megan, that sounds nice and romantic."

Megan's face lit up with a smile. Ms. Purlasky set a cup of coffee in front of Waverly.

"Megan and I found a real nice center to have her wedding at. It's small but lovely. The back area has a beautiful pond, and there are dozens of flowers and shrubbery planted on the grounds. The back of the center's building has a beautiful stone wall with a little ivy growing down it, and there are beautiful white wrought iron benches everywhere back there. It cost just a little over our budget to rent for two hours, but we worked a little extra to help us pay for it. Her reception will be inside the Center, it's huge and nicely decorated."

"Mommy is making my wedding gown. She is an excellent seamstress! Look, I have pictures of it!" Megan quickly pulled out her cell phone to show Waverly a picture of her wedding gown.

"Oh, Megan, it's absolutely stunning! All that beautiful lace at the top and it has tiny pearls going down the sleeves."

Waverly glanced up at Ms. Purlasky. "You are making this?" Waverly couldn't believe it!

"Yes, I am, and what's more, when I'm done with it, it's going to look even better than the one in the picture!"

"Wow! You two are amazing. What can't you do?" Megan looked up at her mother.

"Mommy and I have had to learn to survive for years on our own, Dr. Berman. You pick up a lot of skills fast when you have to pay bills and put food on the table."

"I understand, Megan. Where are you guys going on your honeymoon? Do you know?"

"Kerry knows I want to go to Italy, so I'm hoping." Waverly looked at both Megan and her mother with admiration and then took a sip of her coffee.

"Knock-knock!" Jermaine said as he walked in the kitchen door to the Berman home.

"Good morning, Jermaine, come on in. Bray is ready. Where are you taking him today?"

"Good morning, Dr. Berman."

"Oh, I'm sorry. Jermaine, this is Ms. Purlasky and her daughter, Megan. They are dear friends of mine."

"Ms. Purlasky, Megan, this handsome young man standing in front of you is Jermaine, Bray's best friend."

Ms. Purlasky walked over to Jermaine. "Yes, he is indeed a handsome one, but he needs a little meat on his bones. Why don't you sit down, son, and let me make you a plate of bacon and eggs?"

Jermaine laughed. "Thank you, Ms. Purlasky, but I'm taking Bray out to breakfast this morning. Hey, but I'll take you up on that offer the next time. It was nice meeting you, ladies." Jermaine smiled and headed for Bray's room.

"Hey, hey!"

"Hey, J! I'm ready, man!"

"Okay, let's go!" Jermaine expertly pulled Bray's wheelchair from the window where he had been sitting and looking out. He rolled him into the living room and out the front door effortlessly. When they got to Jermaine's truck, Jermaine opened the passenger side of his truck and said to Bray, "Okay, we are going to do this on the count of three, you ready?"

"Yep!"

Jermaine lifted Bray from the wheelchair and, with Bray's help, was able to get him in his truck without a hitch. Jermaine exhaled heavily after getting Bray settled in the seat and then put his hands on his hips and looked at Bray. "No more burgers for you, man. Salads from now on." They both laughed. Jermaine folded up Bray's wheelchair and stuck it in the back of his truck with a little effort since his jeep was not as big as he thought it was. Jermaine jumped into the truck and pulled off.

*****

After Jermaine and Bray finished their breakfast at the mall food court, Jermaine got up and emptied both of their trays into the trash. "Where to first, Bray? You want to look at clothes, jewelry, name it, man! I got you covered today. We have time, the movie you want to see doesn't start until three, so we are good on time."

"I don't want you to pay for everything today, J. I've got money. My graduation money."

"So do I, I'm good, Bray. Like I said, I've got you today!"

"Do you mind if we stop in the jewelry store over there. I don't need a watch right now, but I'd like to look."

"Sure, let's go!" Jermaine wheeled Bray in the direction of the jewelry store.

"J, hey, J!" Jermaine and Bray turned around to stare in the face of Justin Holston. Justin was a former basketball teammate from high school. Justin stopped suddenly when he noticed Bray in the wheelchair. "Hey, Bray," he said nervously.

"What's up, Justin? How have you been?"

"Bray, hey, man. You know I've been meaning to call, stop by, and see you, but…"

"But you didn't," Bray looked up at Jermaine as he said this.

"I'm sorry, I've just been so busy."

"It's okay, Justin, I understand, man. We all get busy!"

"You know that's true, Bray, we all get busy. But you know what? Me personally, I never get too busy to check on a former teammate, especially if I know he is up against something. But hey, that's just me," Jermaine said while glaring at Justin. Justin gave Jermaine a weak smile. Jermaine and Bray waited to see if there was something more Justin wanted to say, and when he didn't, Jermaine looked down at Bray. "Come on, Bray, let's go. We've got things to do today. Justin is a busy man, so let's send him on his way. Later, Justin."

"Yeah, later, guys."

Jermaine wheeled Bray up to the watch counter once they made it to the jewelry store. "Oh man, Bray! Check out that Bradley Edge Mesh in blue. That thing is awesome!"

"Whoa! You are right, J, nice, very nice!"

"You like it!"

"Man, I love it, but I don't have that kind of money. But like I said, it's nice, J!" They looked at a few more watches before turning to leave the store. In order to exit the jewelry store, Jermaine had to wheel Bray past the engagement rings. "Hey J, can we stop here for a minute, please?"

"Sure, Bray!" Jermaine wheeled Bray closer to the counter to have a look at the engagement rings. As Bray looked at the engagement rings, images of him and Dylan came to mind. Images of them having lunch together in DeMassi High's cafeteria, images of them holding hands at a movie on a Sunday afternoon, images of them running the track together, and images of the day they first met. The day she walked up to him after a basketball game. He shook his head to dismiss the images, but they would not go away that easily. *This isn't right, it's not fair*, Bray thought. Jermaine put his hand on Bray's shoulder. "You okay, Bray?"

"Yeah, J, let's go."

After Bray and Jermaine looked in a few more stores and grabbed a little lunch, it was time to head to the movie theater. As they were moving toward the entrance of the theater, Dylan and Jessica were walking toward them. Jermaine stopped and looked at Dylan. "What's up, Dylan?"

"Hey, J, Bray."

Dylan couldn't pull her eyes away from Bray; as hard as she tried to act nonchalant about seeing him, she couldn't take her eyes off him. "Guys, this is my Aunt Jess. Aunt Jess, this is Jermaine and Bray. They are both good…friends of mine." Dylan patted her hair. "Look, Aunt Jess, my curls have fallen now." Even though Dylan was talking to Jessica, she was still looking at Bray.

"Hello, Jermaine, Bray. Nice to meet you. I've heard a lot about both of you, especially you, Bray. Cree has shared a lot with me concerning you." Jessica looked at Jermaine and smiled and then looked at Bray, but the smile had faded. After all, she wasn't one to try and fake it. If something or someone annoyed her, she did not try to hide it.

Jessica's heart broke for Bray; still, she didn't understand how he couldn't see how much Dylan cared for him. Dylan was practically throwing herself at him, and he wasn't even trying to notice her.

"I'm sorry, Bray and Jermaine, excuse me for one second." Jessica turned to Dylan. "Hey, sweetie, since there seems to be nothing else you see here today that you like, why don't we go back to that shoe store and buy those hot shoes you saw? Plus, that little sales guy was cute as I don't know what, and I noticed him checking you out. I think he likes you, so I'm sure he will give you a big discount! What was his name again, Dylan?" Dylan looked down at the floor. "Dylan, his name?" Jessica said.

Dylan looked at Bray and said so low no one could hear her, "Mike, his name is Mike."

"I'm sorry, Dylan, what was his name again? I'm sorry, I didn't hear you that time," Jessica said with a big smile on her face. This time, Dylan spoke louder, her eyes still glued to Bray.

"I said his name is Mike."

"Oh, that's what I thought you said. Let's go back to that store and see Mike, get those hot shoes you like so much! They looked amazing on you! I mean, how could they not look great on you with that cute little figure of yours!"

Jessica turned to Bray and Jermaine. "It was nice meeting you guys in the flesh. Bray, I'll be stopping by to see you. Enjoy your day. Let's go, Dylan." Jermaine looked at Jessica as she and Dylan walked off.

"Who was that and where did she come from? Man, she is so hot I thought she would set this mall on fire!" Bray rolled his eyes out of frustration.

"Come on, J, the movie will be starting soon."

Chapter 18

Robbie sat at his desk looking at pictures of the car, Waverly's car. The car Bray was cut from the night of his accident. He knew the car belonged to Waverly but had never paid much attention to the color of it, bright red. He looked at the pictures more closely, studied them before calling over his partner, Adam Long, to have a look at them too. "Adam, take a look at this, will you?" Adam walked over and looked at the pictures.

"The Berman kid's accident?"

"Yeah, the car is a bright red. My thinking is, if we can find something on Lombar Road with this same paint color on it, we may be able to match it up to the color of this car. A rearview mirror, a torn-off piece of a door, something from the car that hit Bray with this bright red paint color on it. Maybe then, just maybe, we will finally be on the right track to finding out who hit Bray that night." Adam picked up one of the pictures and took a closer look at it.

"You know, Robbie, I think you might be on to something."

"I sure hope so, Adam, I sure hope so!"

"Hi, Dad, Officer Long," Jermaine said as he walked in the door.

"Hey, Jermaine, what's going on, son?"

"Dad, do you really have to ask? I just dropped Bray off at home. We hung out at the mall together today. He may not be sick of being in the house, but I am sick of him having to be in the house. I had to get him out of there before I went crazy, even if it was for just a little while. We had fun, just like old times. What's going on here, any news?" Robbie took a folder and covered up the photos of Waverly's smashed-up car. He didn't want to incite Jermaine to anything. Not to asking questions, not to getting angry, nothing!

"Not much, son, you know, we are still working hard to come up with a lead on Bray's accident." Jermaine shook his head out of frustration.

"Come on, Dad, how hard can this be? We are living in Taverston, Virginia, not LA! The crime rate here is next to zero. That doesn't give you guys a lot to be concerned about as far as the crime here."

"Jermaine!"

"I know, I know! You're working on it. Well, will you please work on it a little harder! I'm heading home. Good night, Officer Long."

Adam watched Jermaine as he walked out, "He is a pretty upset young man, your son. But you know, he has a good point, Robbie. Why are we having such a hard time with this? There is not a clue, nothing from that night! Not another car, a blown-out tire, nothing! I don't understand it. Did the person that hit Bray just drive off? Are they alive, what?"

"I don't know, Adam, I don't know. I have heard of car accidents where the driver responsible for hitting the other car has just driven off with as little as a scratch, while the car they hit was totaled and the person in it seriously injured."

As Jermaine was driving home, he thought about Bray and Dylan. Dylan still cared very much for Bray, he saw it in her eyes today. "This whole situation sucks," Jermaine said to himself. He then added, "Nobody wins in a situation like this, even if one of the people involved in the accident was able to get up and miraculously walk away from it. More than likely the other person was seriously injured or killed."

*****

Noel and TJ sat on the bottom of Noel's bed and tried to remember the last time they had the Monday Night Chat Session. "You know, Noi, maybe now we need to have our Monday Night Chat Sessions more than ever. Pretty soon Bray, Jermaine, and Dylan will become occupied with college, and we won't all be together. It won't be the same. And with Bray's accident, we need to talk to each other. I know we are all dealing with it as best we can, but maybe a chat session will help us deal with it even better? It would be a good opportunity for Bray to say how he is feeling about the accident."

Noi got up and walked to the desk in her room and sat down. "I don't know, TJ. There are so many things I don't know anymore, understand. Like, why is it taking Officer McBride so long to find the person who hit Bray? Why does Bray refuse to talk about the night of his accident?"

"You mean, he still doesn't want to talk about it?"

"Nope! My parents seem to think he knows who hit him but won't say."

"Oh my god! Are you serious?"

TJ heard her cell phone go off, indicating she had a text message. She looked at it.

"Noi, it's my mom, wanting to know what time I'll be home. Are you okay? Do you need me to stay over tonight? I could if you want me to. Do you need to talk about this further?"

"No, TJ, thanks, I'm okay. You'd better head home, it's getting late." TJ walked over and hugged Noel.

"Good night, Noi. I'll call tomorrow."

"Night, TJ."

As soon as TJ walked out of Noel's room, Ellis walked in. "Hey, Noi, can we talk?"

"Sure, Ellis, what's up?"

"Do you think...do you think Bray will ever walk again?" Noel looked at Ellis, not knowing how to respond to what he'd just asked her.

"Ellis, I would love to say that the day will come when we will see Bray walk again. But the truth is, I don't know." Noel looked down at the floor. "According to what Mom said about his injuries...no, Bray is not going to walk again."

Ellis leaned his back against the wall. "I wish it was me."

"What?"

"I said I wish it was me, not Bray, in that wheelchair. Bray doesn't deserve that, Noi, he is the good son. Never gave Mom and Dad a bit of trouble. He did everything right. Yet he is the one paralyzed and in a wheelchair."

"Ellis, no! Please don't say that! No one deserves to be confined to a wheelchair. Things just happen sometimes. Things that are beyond our control. Hey, Ellis, have you noticed that ever since Bray's accident, Dad has been coming home on time and he seems to be drinking less and less. You know what, I can't even remember the last time I saw him drunk, can you?"

"I don't know, Noi, I haven't been paying Dad too much attention. I'm still trying to find a way to deal with what Bray is going through."

"Ellis, Bray is going to be okay, he is! You just have to believe that. He is going to be fine. We are going to be fine, our family!"

"I heard Mom talking on the phone to Officer McBride. She was asking him if there was anything else she can help them with that will help find the person who hit Bray. I heard her say to him that she thinks Bray knows who hit him."

"Ellis, go to bed. Leave it alone for tonight, okay? You need some rest. We will talk more later." Ellis slowly turned around, opened the door, and walked out of Noel's room. Waverly was standing in the hall outside of Noel's room.

"Mom, how long have you been standing there?"

"Long enough to hear what Noel just told you, Ellis. She is right, you know, we are going to be okay, Ellis, we are! Get some sleep now, son."

Chapter 19

"You are doing great, Jess! Your tests came back free of any trace of cancer."

"Are you serious?"

"Would I kid about something like that? Seriously, you're doing great! Cree hesitated, "Jess, I need to ask you something."

"Cree, why are you looking so serious? What's wrong?"

"Waverly received an envelope. No return address, no signature, and there was fifty-thousand-dollars in cash in that envelope. You know anything about that?"

"And if I do?"

"If you do, you do. If that's the case, I think you need to let Waverly know the money came from you."

"Why, what's the point?"

"I just think she needs to know what a great person you are." Cree smiled at Jessica. "I know it was you, Jess. That was a very kind thing to do, and her family could really use the money."

Jessica walked over and stood in front of Cree. "Thank you, but please will you just let this be our little secret? She needs help and Bray needs a nurse. That fifty-thousand should more than cover the cost of a nurse for Bray for a very long time. Please, Cree, I just want to help, that's all. So not a word to Waverly?" Cree smiled.

"Okay and, Jess?"

"Yes?"

"Thank you."

"Don't mention it."

"Are you up for lunch? Do you have time, any scheduled surgeries?"

"Sorry, I have three scheduled surgeries this afternoon. But what about dinner? Maybe Waverly can join us."

"That sounds great!"

"You know what, Waverly's backyard is amazing! All kinds of flowers in bloom back there right now, and the lake is beautiful! What do you say, meet at Waverly's house at, say, six thirty?"

"I'll be there Cree."

"Okay, I'm going to call her in a bit and let her know we are coming. I will pick up some steaks, and we can put them on the grill." Jessica's face lit up before saying, "I will toss a salad and make some brown rice. This way Waverly won't have to lift a finger." Cree crossed her arms and looked at Jessica. "You really have changed."

"And you are really starting to like me again whether you're willing to admit it or not."

"See you tonight, Jess. Got to go!"

*****

"You know, you would get there a lot quicker if you would just run down the hall."

Cree was rushing to get to the eleventh floor. One of her scheduled surgeries was pushed up an hour according to a message she'd just received on her phone. "Kerry, hey, I'm sorry, I'm in a bit of a hurry. I have a surgery in about thirty minutes. How are you? And congratulations on your engagement. Megan is lovely, and if you hurt her, I'll forget I'm a doctor and kill you." They both laughed.

"How are you, Cree?"

"I'm okay, you know. Just keeping busy and trying to take care of Dylan."

"How is Dylan? I understand that she and Bray are dating."

"*Were* dating."

"I'm sorry to hear that."

"Yeah, so am I. I don't really know what to do about the situation. I know Dylan loves Bray very much and she is trying, but he keeps pushing her away."

"Look, Cree, don't stress over it too much. Dylan and Bray are young, have their whole life ahead of them. If it's meant to be, they will work it out."

"I guess you're right."

"Waverly, how is she holding up?"

"I'm not sure. Sometimes she seems to be all right and then sometimes I catch her just staring off into space."

"Do they have any idea who hit Bray yet?"

"No, and that's what's so troubling. In addition to that, Kerry, Waverly and Nevin seem to think Bray knows who hit him but refuses to say."

"Cree, maybe he doesn't know. Maybe he can't remember a lot about that night, the night of the accident. Bray sustained a lot of injuries in that accident, including mild injuries to the head. He is going to need time."

"Yeah, you're right. Still, I just wish we knew a lot more by now." Cree glanced down at her watch. "Kerry, I'm really sorry but I've got to get going. It was good to see you and congratulations again. All the best to you and Megan."

"Thank you, Cree."

*****

"Everything is just about ready; the salad is tossed and the wine poured. Oh, I forgot the rice."

"No, Jessica, sit. I'll get it."

"Okay. Have you heard from Cree? I wonder where she is with the steaks. It's getting late. When we talked earlier, she said she was on her way."

Waverly froze; she stood in the doorway with the bowl of rice in her hands.

"Waverly, what's wrong? What is it?"

"Jessica, call her, please. Please call Cree right now." Jessica looked at her; she was getting nervous.

"Waverly, what is it? Is something wrong?"

"Bray said those same words to me the night of his accident. He told me he was on his way and the next thing I knew he was in an operating room, fighting for his life!

Please call Cree right now! I need to know! I need to know she is okay!"

Jessica was now beginning to get worried herself. She jumped up and ran into the house and fished out her cell phone. She tapped Cree's number on her contact list and waited for her to answer. "Come on, Cree, answer! Answer the freaking phone!" Waverly walked in and stared at her.

"Did she answer?" Jessica didn't respond; she just kept trying to call Cree. There was still no answer. Jessica began to pace back and forth. "Okay, okay…let's just calm down. I mean, she is only an hour or so late. Wine, where is the wine? We could both use a glass. Waverly, why did you do this? Why did you get me all crazy like this? I'm about to lose it! Dylan, I'll call Dylan."

"Jessica, no! We can't call Dylan. We will get her all worried and scared."

Jessica grabbed her bag and car keys and headed for the door!

"Jess, where are you going?"

"Out to look for her. This is not like Cree. She is never late for anything, and if she is, she calls or texts. It's going on over an hour now. She is not answering her phone!"

"Jessica, just hold on a minute. Slow down, I'm sorry. I should not have put thoughts in your head, thoughts that something may have happened to Cree. Look, let's just go back on the deck, sit down, relax, and have a glass of wine."

Waverly poured herself a glass of wine and then poured a glass for Jessica. "I think I'm going to need a second glass of wine, Waverly, so you might as well go ahead and pour it now."

"Are you serious?"

"Yes, you did this. My being crazy right now is all your fault!" Waverly burst out laughing and poured Jessica a second glass of wine. Waverly walked over to the edge of the deck and looked at the lake.

"You know, when I first met Cree, I thought to myself, what a lovely woman, but still I was a little envious of her. When she started working at Simon Memorial, she had already been appointed as head of surgery. The job I thought I would get, had worked hard to get. The better I got to know her, the more my respect and admiration grew for her. She was amazing in the operating room and still is. Her bedside manner is matchless. She is an excellent doctor. I love her, our friendship means the world to me."

"I know what you mean, Cree is special. When she got pregnant with Dylan, everyone thought she would crumble, give up on everything. But I knew better, not Cree. Not the Cree I know. She fought hard to get into medical school, and when she did, she immersed herself in her studies. She was relentless in her determination to graduate at the top of her class. There was no stopping her, her motivator being Dylan, wanting to provide for and take care of her. She never gave up, and now it's paid off. I love her, too, and I am so glad to have her back in my life. And I'm glad we've become friends, Waverly."

"Hey, guys," Cree said as she rushed onto the deck and tossed her bag in an empty chair. "Sorry I'm late. I had to stop off and pick up the steaks. The store was packed, but I got them. Then traffic was horrible." Waverly and Jessica just looked at Cree and said nothing. "What's wrong with you guys? Why are you looking at me like that?"

"We are just glad to see you, Cree, that's all," Jessica said.

"I'm glad to see you guys too! I've got the steaks, so let's toss these babies on the grill." Jessica walked over and took the steaks out of Cree's hands.

"You rest, I'll put these on the grill."

"Oh my goodness! Cree was right, Waverly," Jessica said as she stepped down into the yard to reach the grill. "It is absolutely breathtaking back here. The yard, the lake! I could spend hours out here just thinking and dreaming."

"Thank you, Jessica. You know you are free to stop by anytime and just hang out on the deck with me."

Jessica smiled and said, "Oh, I'm counting on doing that."

Waverly turned to Cree and sliced another piece of her steak off to eat. "How did your surgeries go today?"

"Not bad," Cree said after swallowing a forkful of salad. I did have a little bit of a struggle with one patient, only because her blood pressure for some reason dropped too low before I could get her stitched back up. But we hung in there and were able to close her up without problems."

"Waverly and I have a confession to make. When you didn't show up on time, we got very worried. You should have seen us, it was insane."

"I'm really sorry, I tried to get here as soon as I could."

"No, Cree, it's not you. It's just that ever since Bray's accident, I've been a little on edge. You know, Nevin and I were thinking that maybe Bray should see someone. I'm beginning to think I need to see someone. I'm trying really hard every single day, but I don't know if I'm doing any better than I was when Bray's accident first happened."

Cree got up and walked to the kitchen to put on a pot of coffee and then walked back and stood in the doorway. "Waverly, you are doing great. Honestly, I don't know how you are doing it, but you are. You're tough, I've seen you stand up under immeasurable pressure in the operating room, and you kicked butt!"

"Waverly, I think what Cree is trying to say is, we're proud of you. When I first met you in Dad's restaurant that night having dinner with Cree, you gave the appearance of not being too strong, but you've proven me wrong. I'm going to start cleaning off the table."

"No, Jessica, you have quite a way to drive in order to get home. I will stay here with Waverly and help clean up."

"Are you sure?"

"Yes, of course, and text us when you get in, okay?"

"All right, I will. Good night." Waverly and Cree said good night to Jessica and started cleaning off the table.

"Waverly, can I talk to you about something?"

"Of course, what's going on, Cree?"

"Dylan is having a really tough time with this, with the accident. She tries to pretend that she is all right, but I know she isn't. In a few weeks, she will be heading to medical school, and I'd like to think that she and Bray have come to some type of an agreement about their future before she leaves here."

"Cree, Bray, and Dylan are so young. Honestly, I don't know if they even know what they really want."

"Dylan loves Bray, Waverly, I know she does. I'm just so sorry it happened, the accident. So much has changed now."

*****

There was a breeze coming through the window as Bray sat in his room and stared out at the day. He wished he could go on the court in his backyard, dribble around a little, and make a few shots into the basket. It was a perfect day to shoot around on the court, something he hadn't done in a while. He missed basketball, missed the sound of his teammates cheering him on and the thrill of making that three-point shot that would win the victory game for Raymond DeMassi High School. "Those were the good old days," he said to himself.

Bray pondered over the fact that sooner or later, he would have to answer Officer McBride's questions about his car accident. He'd managed to avoid not only his questions but his mother's and Jermaine's questions as well regarding that night. The night his father hit him head-on on Lombar Road. *How long am I going to be able to hold on to this secret before it finally destroys me?* He needed to talk to someone, needed to clear his conscience, but if he did, what would be the consequences for his dad, his family? Question after question formed in his head until they collided, causing him to have a massive headache.

Dylan, they needed to talk. He needed to somehow convince her that things would never be the same between them again. The thought of her spending the rest of her life with someone else was torture at its best. He didn't know which was more painful, the fact that his own father had caused him to become partially paralyzed or the thought of Dylan picking out furniture for a house she would share with a husband other than him. So many situations to be faced and so little time to figure out how to face them. His headache worsened.

Bray turned his wheelchair away from the window, pulled his cell phone out, and called Dylan. He waited for Dylan to answer, and when she did, he almost hung up on her, feeling there was no way he could go through with what he was about to.

"Dylan, it's Bray."

"Hey! I know it's you, Bray. There is no way I could ever forget your voice. How are you? You okay? Do you need me to come over? I can be there in less than twenty minutes!"

"Yeah, I need you to come over. I mean, we need to talk." Dylan took her cell phone away from her ear and looked at it; she was nervous, scared even. She put the phone back up to her ear.

"Okay, I'm on my way. Bray?"

"Yeah, Dylan?"

"I love you."

"I'll see you when you get here, Dylan. Drive safely."

About twenty minutes later, Dylan drove up in front of the Berman home and parked her car. She sat in it for a few minutes, trying to get control of her emotions. She pulled out her lipstick and used her car mirror to smooth a little on. "Okay, here we go. Just stop thinking the worst and you will be able to get out of this car," she said to herself. She picked up the cupcakes she'd stopped off at the bakery to get for Bray and looked in the box at them. She wanted them to be perfect, no smeared icing; each cupcake had to be perfect.

When she knocked on the door, Waverly answered, "Dylan, hi honey. How are you?"

"Hello, Dr. Berman. Bray called and asked me to come over. I brought cupcakes. Would you like one?" Waverly looked at Dylan and then glanced in the direction of Bray's room.

"Dylan?"

"Please, Dr. Berman, may I go back to see him now?"

"Sure, honey." Waverly slowly stepped aside to let Dylan in.

"Bray?"

"Hey, Dylan, come in and close the door behind you, please."

"Sure. I stopped off at the bakery and picked you up some cupcakes. Would you like one now? I have napkins."

"Dylan, what I'm about to say to you is going to be very difficult, so please let me finish before you try to respond… okay?" Dylan nodded her head in agreement. "Dylan, I'm seeing someone else now." Dylan started breathing heavily and then willed herself to calm down, but it wasn't working.

"What?"

"I said that I'm seeing someone else now."

"When? How?"

"I met her a week ago while I was at one of my medical appointments."

Dylan couldn't say anything for a few minutes. She set the box of cupcakes down on the bed. "I don't believe you!"

"Dylan…"

"What's her name?"

"Her name is not important."

"No! You love me, Bray, and I know it! Why are you saying these awful things to me?"

"Dylan, I don't know how else to say this to you, so I'm just going to come right out and be point-blank. It's over between us. Move on with your life because I have."

"Bray?"

"I wish you all the best with medical school. You're going to make a great doctor one day."

"I am not leaving this room, Bray, until you tell me the truth!"

"I just did. You just need to accept it. Goodbye, Dylan." Dylan turned and looked out the window and then back at Bray. Without another word, she picked the cupcakes up off the bed, walked over to the trash can and tossed them in, and then walked out.

After Waverly was sure Dylan was gone, she walked to Bray's room and stood in his doorway. "Bray, son, what have you done? I heard what you said to Dylan, and you and I both know not a word of it is true."

"I did what needed to be done, Mom. Dylan would have never let go on her own. She needed something to help her let go!"

"You lied to her, Bray, and that is inexcusable and unacceptable! Lying, there is no benefit in doing so, Bray! You tell one lie, sooner or later you're going to have to tell a second one to cover the first lie up. Then a third and fourth lie until your story becomes so confused you don't know what to say. Let me tell you something, son. Never allow yourself to become comfortable with lying. It will destroy you if you do in so many ways. Find a way, Bray, find a way to fix this, or so help me I will go to Dylan and tell her the truth myself!" Bray shook his head slowly.

"I'm sorry I lied, I'm sorry, but I didn't know what else to do! I don't want her to go on thinking that one day we will get married. I didn't want to wind up hurting her." Waverly looked at Bray and walked into his room so he could see the seriousness of what she was about to say.

"You didn't want to wind up hurting her. Well, I've got news for you, Bray, you just did."

Chapter 20

Jermaine bent over and tried to catch his breath. He'd just jogged three miles, and the last time he ran, he was barely able to complete one mile. He had intentionally run until he reached Lombar Road. It was earlier in the day, which meant more daylight. He walked to the edge of the road leading to the woods and then turned around suddenly; the license plate, where was it? He'd seen it the last time he was there. *Maybe it has a connection to Bray's accident*, he thought.

He started walking down Lombar Road and began to search the ground, still trying to remember exactly where he'd seen the license plate. The farther he walked, the more exhausted he became, but he was determined to find that license plate. He heard a car pulling up beside him.

"Dad?"

"Hey, J, what are you doing out here, son?"

"I went for a run, and this is where I wound up, big surprise!"

"Jermaine, you need to leave Bray's accident investigation to the police. Trust me, we are doing everything within our power to learn what happened, who hit Bray. Was he somehow at fault?"

"What! Dad, you can't be serious! You don't honestly believe what you just said could be true?"

"What?"

"That Bray could have somehow been at fault for the accident."

"Jermaine, we don't know exactly what happened. We are searching for answers, clues."

"That's exactly why I'm out here, Dad. Searching for answers, looking for clues. I don't believe for a half a second that Bray was at fault for his accident!"

"Come on, son, I'll give you a ride home."

"No thanks, I'll jog home."

Robbie reluctantly pulled off and hoped Jermaine would start home soon. Lombar Road was tricky. Cars traveled that road all day long, and accidents happened on that road all night long. He looked in his rearview mirror to see if Jermaine was even thinking about leaving, heading home. He wasn't; he had started to walk up and down the road again, keeping his eyes glued to the ground.

Jermaine pulled out his cell phone and sent Bray a message. "Bray, the car that hit you on Lombar Road the night of your accident, do you remember what color it was?" Jermaine kept glancing down at his phone; almost thirty minutes passed with no reply from Bray. He started walking up and down the road again, picking up pieces of glass, rocks, gadgets he didn't even recognize and then tossing them back to the ground when he concluded they were of no use in helping learn who hit Bray. He sent Bray another text, "Bray, where are you? I need an answer to that last text, man."

Six minutes later, Bray replied, "Where are you, J? Why do you need to know what color the car was? I've already told you all I can tell."

Jermaine looked down at his phone and then swore under his breath. "Okay, Bray, later."

*****

"Dylan, I'm home and I've brought pizza, the real cheesy kind that you like!" Cree walked to the kitchen and put the pizza down and then went in to use the bathroom. When she came back out, she called for Dylan again. "Dylan, where are you?" She walked to her bedroom and peeped in, but she wasn't there. Cree heard the back door opening. "Dylan, is that you?"

"Yeah, Mom, hi." Cree walked swiftly to the kitchen to see Dylan.

"Hi, honey, where have you been?"

"I went for a run, Mom. The pizza looks good, and I'm really hungry. If you will excuse me, I'm going to take a quick shower. I'll be right back." Cree turned and looked at Dylan as she walked out of the room. She then went to the fridge and pulled out fixings for a salad. When Dylan returned, they sat down to eat.

"Dylan, what is it?"

"What do you mean?"

"What's on your mind? What's bothering you? Please don't tell me it's nothing because I know something is. Is it Bray? Did you see or talk to him today?"

"Yeah, I did."

"And?"

Silence hung in the air between them. "Dylan?"

"He is seeing someone else now, so I guess it's time for me to move on."

Cree reached over and touched Dylan's hand. "Dylan, I'm so sorry. I don't understand this, how is it that Bray could be seeing someone else? How?"

"Seems he met her while at one of his medical appointments."

"Do we know her?"

"I don't know, he wouldn't tell me her name."

"Dylan, I need to share something with you."

"Yes, what is it?"

"Dylan, maybe this has happened for the best."

"What do you mean?"

"A lot has changed. Maybe it's to your advantage that Bray feels the way he does. This way you won't have to hurt him once you go off to college and meet someone else."

"Meet someone else? What are you talking about? There is no one else. Bray and I promised each other that after we graduated college, we would get jobs, find a place to live in, and get married. There is no someone else in that equation, Mom."

"Dylan, Bray has left you no choice."

Cree's cell phone rang; it was Jessica. "What are you up to? I thought I would stop by and bring some amazing French desserts. Okay with you?"

"Jess, now is not a good time."

"Why not? Cree, what's going on?" *The old Jessica is coming out*, Cree thought.

"It's Dylan, she's...she's not feeling very well right now."

"What's wrong with her?"

"It's a long story, but for now, I need to get back to her. I'll call you tomorrow."

"Cree, I want to come over. Maybe I can help."

"I really appreciate you wanting to help, Jess, really I do, but this is something Dylan and I must work out. Good night, I'll call you tomorrow." Jessica didn't respond.

Forty-five minutes later, Jessica knocked on Cree's door. Cree opened the door. "I thought I told you…"

"Yeah, yeah, yeah, and yeah! I know what you told me, but when have you ever known me to listen to anything or anyone unless I want to? Where is Dylan?"

"She is in her room, sleeping now."

"Bray?"

"Yep."

"Men!"

"Jess, Bray is seventeen years old and he is going through a lot right now."

"So what's up?"

"He told Dylan he is seeing someone else."

"Well, is he?"

"I don't know, but I honestly don't think so."

"Then why did he say that to her?"

"Jessica, Bray is a wonderful young man. He is handsome, smart, and caring. I have no doubt that he cares for Dylan, to what extent, I can't say. But I honestly believe that his now being confined to a wheelchair has something to do with him telling Dylan that today. I think he only told her that to get her to stop holding out hope that one day they will be married. He cared enough for her to want to see her happy. I don't condone lying under any circumstance, but I think it was the only way he knew how to push her away from him once and for all."

"This really stinks! And why can't the police find who caused his accident? It's been a while now. What are they doing about this?"

"I wish I knew the answer to that question."

"Cree, maybe it's time to call in a private investigator."

"Jess, Waverly's family doesn't have the money for that right now."

Jessica got up and walked to the middle of the room before looking at Cree and saying, "I do."

"Jessica, you've already put out so much money to help them, and it was so thoughtful and kind of you to do that. But I'm sure Waverly would not want you to keep going into your bank account and withdrawing money to help them."

"Who said I was going into my bank account? I'm not *that* nice! I'm going into Dad's account, I have access to it. Trust me, the man has more money than he can ever spend in this lifetime. He won't miss it. I've got a brilliant idea!"

"Jess?"

"No, really, I do! We haven't done anything for the graduates, right?" Cree thought for a second.

"No, we haven't. I guess everyone has been so concerned for Bray and his family we all just forgot about it."

"Well, Saturday I'm throwing a cookout for them at my house that they will love! I'm having the pool cleaned today incidentally, so it will be ready. Just leave everything to me. Saturday at five? Are you free?"

"Yeah, I am, I'm off every other Saturday. Oh, but wait! Dylan and I are driving up to VCU School of Medicine to meet her roommate and check out the grounds."

"And you didn't invite me?"

"Jess, you are more than welcome to join us if you'd like. We are leaving around ten."

"Great, I'm coming with you! So the cookout can be Sunday. Text me names and numbers of people you'd like to invite, and I will do the rest."

*****

Jessica was beyond tired when Sunday, the day of the cookout, came. The trip to Virginia Commonwealth University was nice and fun. However, she, Cree, and Dylan had walked forever so it seemed around the grounds and had eaten way too many rich foods. They all loved Dylan's room and roommate. Cree and Dylan chatted with Gabrielle Mason, Dylan's roommate. While they had chatted with Gabrielle, Jessica busied herself making notes of all the things she was going to buy for Dylan and her room.

After fluffing a few throw pillows, Jessica ran to her backyard and started questioning the cooks she'd hired to take care of the food and the grills. "Do we have enough ribs? What about the crab cakes? Who is taking care of those? They must be right! Nothing worse than a horrible and too bready crab cake. They are all meat, right, Craig?"

Craig was the cook in charge of the food and making sure it was cooked and grilled to perfection. He worked in Jessica's father's restaurant and he was the best!

"Yes, Miss Jessica, we are doing great! There are plenty of hot dogs, burgers, fish, corn on the cob, the salads are ready, the drinks are ready! We are good to go!"

"Great!"

Before Craig could finish sharing other information with her about the food, Jessica glanced over at the DJ. She walked over to him after she and Craig finished talking and smiled. "Hey, how is it going?"

"Hey, it's going great!"

"You've got some good music, right? I mean you know what teenagers listen to these days, I'm sure."

"Without a doubt. I'll keep them up and dancing, no question!" Jessica gave the DJ a thumbs-up and walked off.

Before rushing up to her room to get dressed, she glanced over at the large graduation pictures of Dylan, Bray, and Jermaine. She'd used the graduation pictures Cree had been able to get for her and had them blown up, renting three easels to rest them on. "You guys are beautiful," Jessica said to herself as she stared at their pictures. Her eyes lingering on Bray's picture, she swallowed back emotion. She hurt not just for Bray but also for Dylan. *Don't worry, Bray and Dylan, it's going to happen for you two. I'm determined to make it happen. Seeing someone else, Bray, I think not.* Jessica turned away from the pictures and ran up to her room to get dressed.

Ms. Purlasky, Megan and Kerry were the first to arrive at the cookout. They all got out and looked up at Jessica's home in amazement. "Are we at the right address?"

"I don't know, Kerry, I think so," Megan said. Ms. Purlasky looked at Jessica's house.

"A waste, an absolute waste! Cree said Jessica lives alone, so why is she living in a castle?"

"Mommy, please, it's not a castle. Please don't start. Be nice, we are guests here. Now be nice, please."

Ms. Purlasky looked at Megan and rolled her eyes and then rushed up to Jessica's front door. Kerry and Megan walked slowly behind her hand in hand. Ms. Purlasky stopped and turned around to look at them before saying, "Come quickly. You see each other every day and every night, I would think you would be sick of each other by now."

"Mommy!"

"Oh, don't you Mommy me. Just come, come quickly! It's hot out here!"

Once everyone had arrived at the cookout, Jessica called for everyone's attention. "Listen, everyone! Please listen! Today we are here to celebrate the high school graduation of Dylan, Jermaine, and Bray! Let's give them a huge round of applause. They certainly deserve it!" Everyone broke into applause for Dylan, Jermaine, and Bray!

"Okay, I'm going to point out a few things to you before we get this party started. Look around you, everyone. There is a table of appetizers, a table of pastas and salads, a table of desserts, a table of crabs, and containers full of soft drinks! My friends stationed at the grills, and there are five grills, are ready and waiting for you to walk over and give your request. You have a choice of steaks, salmon, hot dogs, ribs, fish, you name it! There are some hot dogs and burgers ready right now. Oh, I almost forgot, there is also a table of wine and coolers full of beer with two large coolers of ice right beside them.

"Noi, TJ, and Ellis, where are you?" Jessica said while searching the crowd made up of people she invited from back home. People Cree and Waverly worked with at Simon Memorial Hospital and friends from Dylan, Bray, and Jermaine's high school. "Oh, there you guys are. You see the table full of wine and the coolers full of beer?"

Ellis, TJ, and Noel all said, "Yeah!"

Jessica smiled at them before saying, "Stay away from it!" Everyone burst into laughter. Jessica then shouted, "Let's party!"

The cookout was underway, the DJ played music that a few teenagers started dancing to, and even some of the adults joined in. Most of the teenagers ran and jumped in the pool. The adults headed for the grills and the tables of food. Cree walked over to Jessica and smiled at her. "I got to hand it to you, my friend, you really know how to throw a party!" Jessica looked at Cree and winked at her.

"Well, you know what they say, 'Go big or go home!'" They both laughed and headed for one of the grills.

"Let's go, my man, let's go load up that plate of yours," Jermaine said as he walked over and grabbed Bray's wheelchair.

"Hey, J! Mom just went to get me something!"

"Good, she can sit down and eat it herself, relax a little."

Bray laughed and let Jermaine wheel him over to each table he wanted to go to, and then the two of them found a space at a table and enjoyed their food.

Dylan walked over to them. Any other time Jermaine would have said something smart to her, but he didn't this time. He could see the hurt, see that she was suffering. "What's up, Dylan? You look nice. I like the shoes you're rocking."

"Thank you, Aunt Jess bought them for me."

"Nice, hey, I'm going to leave you two for a second, go help myself to a plate of crabs. I'll bring you some back, Bray."

"Okay, thanks, J."

Bray held his empty plate in his hands nervously. Dylan reached down and took it from him and then walked over and tossed it in the trash. She picked up a bunch of napkins from a table on her way back. When she reached Bray, she took the napkins and wiped his mouth and face and then the crumbs off his clothes. "Thanks, Dylan, but I could have done that."

"I know, but I wanted to do it. I want to be the one who takes care of you, Bray, for the rest of your life. No one is going to take care of you like I will. All I'm asking for is a chance. Please give me a chance, Bray, to prove that I can take care of you."

"Dylan, please, this is hard enough." Dylan ignored him.

"Where is your girlfriend, Bray? Why isn't she here, by your side, where she should be." Bray licked his lips and looked down. Jermaine walked up with a plate full of crabs for Bray, and Dylan then turned and walked away.

"Jessica, Jess!" Waverly called to her. Jessica turned from talking to one of the cooks at a grill and motioned for Waverly to come on over.

"Hi!"

"Hi! You look awesome, Jess! Did you color your hair?"

"Yep, I got bored with my old color, so I decided to go with a funky red! You like?"

"I love it!" Waverly said with a smile. "Hey, Jess, I just want to thank you for throwing this cookout for the boys and Dylan."

"Trust, it was my pleasure!"

"Guess what, I've hired a nurse to help with Bray. She passed my interview with flying colors and her references checked out!"

"Wonderful, I'm so happy for you and your family."

"You know, someone sent me fifty-thousand-dollars in cash to help with hiring a nurse."

"Oh really!" Jessica said, pretending to be surprised.

"Really. Jessica, the person who did that is one of a kind. It takes a person with a very kind and thoughtful heart to do something like that. You know, I bet whoever it was is just as beautiful as you are, Jess. If you see anyone that fits the description of the person I just described to you, please tell them I said thank you and share this kiss with them." Waverly smiled at Jessica and then reached up and kissed her on the cheek. "See you later, Jess."

Cree was standing in the distance watching them. After Waverly walked off, Jessica looked up and saw her. Jessica mouthed to Cree, "Did you tell her?" Cree laughed and mouthed back to Jessica while holding up both of her hands in a show of innocence, "Nope, not me."

Jessica looked around the crowd in search of Bray. She saw him sitting over with Jermaine and walked over to them. "Hi, Jermaine, Bray." They both said hi, and Bray shot a quick glance at Jermaine, who had his eyes fixated on Jessica. Jessica turned to Jermaine and smiled. "Would you mind me stealing Bray away from you for a few minutes? I promise to bring him back soon."

"No, I don't mind at all."

"Thank you, Jermaine."

Jessica rolled Bray away from the crowd. Bray was a little puzzled and tried to figure out what was going on. When Jessica found an empty bench, she stopped and sat down. Bray looked at her quizzically. "Are you enjoying the cookout, Bray?"

"Yes ma'am, and thank you for doing this for me and my friends."

"I enjoyed doing this for you guys. Cree tells me you want to be a writer. You know, I've always wanted to be a writer, but my concentration span is too short and I'm too impatient, I get irritated too easily. Writing takes serious concentration and you have to have discipline."

"Yes, it does, but I love to write. I've wanted to be a writer since I was in junior high school. I agree, discipline is very important."

"Well, from what I've heard about you, I know you are going to be a very good writer. Bray, I'm very sorry about your accident and I want you to know that if there is anything, anything at all I can do to help you, you just let me know. Cree has my number, okay?"

"Sure, yes ma'am."

"How are you keeping yourself occupied this summer?" Jessica laughed. "What a crazy question, I mean, you're so handsome I'm sure you have thousands of girls just waiting in line."

Bray smiled shyly and said, "No ma'am."

"No! Well, I understand. You look way too smart to try and juggle a few girls. But a girlfriend, I'm sure you must have a girlfriend?"

Again, Bray smiled shyly and said, "No, ma'am." Dylan came to his mind and he shook his head to erase thoughts of her. Jessica noticed him struggling with something.

"Bray, are you okay?"

"Yes ma'am. Do you mind if we go back now? I'm getting a little tired."

"Of course, honey, I'll take you back right now." Jessica got up and pushed Bray back to where Jermaine sat waiting for him.

It was nearing nine o'clock and getting dark. The lights surrounding the pool and Jessica's backyard automatically switched on as the sun started to set. There were still a few people in the pool, the aroma of barbecue filled the air, and groups of people were huddled together at tables and in small groups, enjoying one another's company and casual conversation.

Jessica walked over to Cree with two tall glasses of wine and handed one to her. "Enjoying yourself?"

"Immensely," Cree responded as she took the glass of wine from Jessica. "I saw you talking to Bray. What's up? Does he have a girlfriend?" Cree asked with a smile.

"Nope," Jessica said and took a sip of her wine.

"Not a word to Dylan, Jess, promise? Let the two of them work it out."

"Do I have to?"

"Yes, you do." Jessica took another sip of her wine.

"Okay, but at least we know there is no girlfriend."

"Yes, we do," Cree said and finished off her glass of wine.

Once the cookout wound down and it got later, everyone started filling their plates with leftovers and helping with cleanup. People could be heard saying how much they enjoyed themselves and that they would not have to cook for a week. Jessica said good night to the last of her guests, turned out the lights, and went up to shower and go to bed.

Chapter 21

Martha Purlasky stared at the stain on the floor of Waverly's kitchen and tried to make out what it was. Megan looked at her mother and let out a heavy sigh. "Mommy, really, you've been staring at that stain on and off for the last twenty minutes. Clean it or leave it."

"I am trying to figure out how it got there. This tile was spotless when we left here last week."

"It's been a week. You didn't expect the floor to look the same as we left it last week, did you?"

"Yes," Ms. Purlasky said matter-of-factly.

"Oh, for goodness' sakes, I will clean it myself," Megan said.

Waverly walked in the kitchen followed by a short dark-haired woman with big eyes and hair cut so close Megan and Ms. Purlasky had to try to figure out the gender. "Megan, Ms. Purlasky, meet Pamela Thompson, Bray's nurse."

"That's Pam, ma'am. I'd like to be called Pam, thank you, please."

"Thank you, please, where are you from, child, speaking like that?" Ms. Purlasky wanted to know.

"Oh yes ma'am, I'm from just seven miles outside of Taverston. My family owns a farm and we sell a lot of our crops to the grocery stores here in Taverston."

Waverly looked at Pam and smiled. "This is Ms. Purlasky and her daughter Megan. They are kind enough to come over and help with the cleaning and cooking on the weekends. I can use all the help I can get. Today is my husband's day to care for Bray, but I've still got grocery shopping and other things to do."

Nevin walked in the kitchen and poured himself a cup of coffee. Ms. Purlasky cleared her throat in an effort to get his attention. Nevin didn't hear her. "There are four women standing here, Mr. Berman. You can greet each of us one at a time or all at once, take your pick."

Nevin turned around to face them. "I'm sorry, Ms. Purlasky, my mind was elsewhere. Good morning, ladies."

"Good morning," they replied.

Pam looked at Nevin and then slowly walked up closer to him to get a better look. "Excuse me, sir, but I think I've seen you somewhere before."

"Who, me?"

"Yes, sir, I think it was at a bar off Lombar Road. I was there with my boyfriend one night, and I remember you because this lady at the bar was really trying to come on to you, but you just ignored her. I remember thinking, now there is a real gentleman." Nevin looked at Waverly, who stood watching him closely, waiting for his response to Pam.

Nevin took a sip of his coffee and shrugged his shoulders. "I guess it could've been me. I do go to that bar sometimes."

"I really think it was you. When my boyfriend and I left the bar that night, we took Lombar Road home and there had been a terrible accident. Did you see it? This car was flipped over in the street. The police had just gotten there."

"No, I don't recall seeing it."

"Well, I just figured you might have since you left the bar just a little before my boyfriend and I did. We watched you, we were concerned, you were drunk. I'm glad to see you made it home all right."

"Yes, thank you. Well, if you ladies will excuse me, I have to check on my son."

"Yes, sir, nice seeing you again."

Waverly watched Nevin walk out of the room. She wanted to follow him and question him about what Pam had just said but decided it best to wait a while. She then turned to Pam. "Pam, the car you saw flipped over on Lombar Road that night belonged to me, I believe. The one driving it was my son, the person you've been hired to care for."

Pam's mouth flew open and she quickly put her hand up to cover it. She then slowly took it down and looked at Waverly sadly. "I'm sorry, Dr. Berman, I am so terribly sorry, I had no idea."

"It's all right, Pam. You couldn't have known that. If you will please follow me, I will take you to Bray." After Pam and Waverly left the kitchen, Megan and Ms. Purlasky looked at each other and slowly shook their heads.

****

Waverly pulled into a parking space outside the grocery store and sat there for a few minutes. She pulled out her cell phone and called Cree. When Cree answered, Waverly had to find her words before saying, "Cree, it's me, Waverly." Cree laughed.

"I know it's you. Waverly, surely you know by now that I have your number saved in my cell." Waverly took so long to respond Cree started to get concerned. "Waverly, are you there? Is everything all right?"

"I'm not sure."

"Waverly, what…what do you mean you are not sure? What's wrong?"

"Cree, the nurse, the nurse hired to care for Bray, she was in the kitchen when Nevin walked in to get coffee. She saw him, she saw him at a bar off Lombar Road the night of Bray's accident. She…she said he was drunk when he left. Then a few minutes after Nevin left, she and her boyfriend left and they took Lombar Road headed home, and that's when they saw it…my car flipped over in the road. Bray was driving it."

Cree was standing in her office, putting some files away. She turned slowly from the file cabinet and walked over to her desk to sit down and took her cell phone off speaker. "Is she sure? Is she sure it was Nevin she saw in the bar?"

"Yes, she even got closer to him to make certain he was the same man she saw in the bar that night." Cree paused.

"Waverly, that doesn't mean anything. Nevin came home that night, right? He was okay?"

"Yeah, but while we were at the hospital that night, I noticed his head had a bandage on it."

"I know what you're thinking, Waverly, and it's insane. Listen to me. Nevin would never hit Bray, his own son, and just leave him there!"

"I don't know what to think or believe anymore, Cree. This is all too much."

"Waverly, it wasn't Nevin who hit Bray, it wasn't! So stop thinking like that. Where are you?"

"I'm at the grocery store. I'll be heading home soon!"

"Okay, just relax. It wasn't Nevin."

"Okay, thanks, Cree."

"Sure." Cree ended the call. She sat at her desk and tried to make some sense of what Waverly had just shared with her and then said to herself, "It wasn't Nevin, it wasn't! He would never hit his own son and just drive off and leave him there."

*****

"Nevin?"

"Yeah, honey, what is it? I'm working on some figures for work."

"May I talk to you for a minute?" Nevin looked up from the pile of papers on his desk in his home office.

"Waverly, I'm sorry. Can this wait?"

"No, it can't." Nevin dropped the papers he was holding, down on the desk, and looked at Waverly.

"What is it? What do you want to talk to me about?"

Waverly didn't know where to begin. "You know, I've noticed that ever since Bray's accident, you haven't been drinking as much, if at all. You're doing great!" Nevin closed his eyes and massaged his forehead before saying,

"Yeah, ever since I learned that whoever hit Bray that night may have been drunk, I get sick to my stomach whenever I try to lift a drink to my mouth."

Bray was wheeling his chair past when he heard Waverly and Nevin talking. He stopped to listen. "Nevin, the night of Bray's accident, you were at that bar off Lombar Road. Remember, Pam said she saw you there. When you left, were you drunk?"

"Hi, Mom, Dad," Bray said as he wheeled himself into Nevin's home office. Waverly turned and looked at him.

"What is it, son? Do you need something?" Nevin asked.

"Yes, as a matter of fact, I do. But I need Mom to help me with it."

"Your mother is tired, Bray. Is it something I can help you with?"

"I'm sorry, Dad, but you don't make blueberry pancakes as good as Mom does. I'm sorry, Mom, I'm hungry. Would you mind?"

"Sure, son, I'll be right there."

Bray didn't move; he stayed in the room. Nevin and Waverly looked at him. "Go on, son, I'll be right there."

"Would you mind coming now, Mom, please? I'm pretty hungry."

"Bray, your mother—"

"It's okay, Nevin, you and I can talk later. Come on, Bray, let's go get you those pancakes."

*****

After taking a sip of his water, Bray ate the last of his blueberry pancakes and glanced over at Waverly, who was washing the dishes. "Mom."

"Yeah, Bray."

"Why does everybody keep asking about my accident? It's over now, what's done is done. I just want to move on from it."

"Bray, it's not that simple."

"Yes, it is. I wish everybody would just leave it alone. I'm trying to."

Noel walked in the kitchen and looked at the stove. "I smell blueberry pancakes. Are there more?"

"I'm sorry, Noi, Bray wanted blueberry pancakes for a little late-night snack tonight. He was still hungry, and they are all gone."

"Hungry! Bray, how could you possibly still have been hungry! You ate, like, fifty plates of baked chicken and rice as well as two large bowls of salad!"

"Noi, leave your brother alone. If he wants blueberry pancakes as a late-night snack, I don't think that's too much to ask. Where is Ellis?"

"He is in his room on the computer." Noel then turned and went back to her room.

"I think I'll go to bed too," Waverly said as she dried the last dish and put it away. "Is there anything else you need, Bray, before I leave?"

"No, Mom, thank you."

"Okay, just let your dad know when you're ready for bed and he will help you tonight, okay?"

"Okay, Mom, and thanks again for the pancakes."

"You're welcome, Bray."

Before wheeling himself back to his room, Bray stopped and peeped in Nevin's office. "You okay, Dad?" Nevin glanced at him.

"Sure, son, why do you ask?"

"I was just wondering. How have you been doing with…with the drinking?"

"I'm doing okay, Bray. As a matter of fact, I was telling your mother earlier that I haven't had a taste for a drink since your accident."

"That's great, Dad, I'm so proud of you. Hey, Dad, remember the time I was seven years old and kept falling off my bike while trying to learn to ride it?"

Nevin laughed. "Of course I do."

"Well, I remember you kept putting me back on it and told me to keep trying, and by the end of the day, I was riding it on my own. I also remember you working two jobs while Mom was in medical school so she could just concentrate on going to school and not have to worry about trying to work too."

Nevin looked at Bray. "Wow, son, you have a great memory. You know, Bray, I may not have been at all your basketball games when you were in high school, but I always want you to remember this too. When everyone else turns their back and walks away from you, I'll still be standing in front of you. I'll be there for you, son, when it counts the most…and that's when no one else is."

"Thanks, Dad."

"You're welcome, Bray."

Chapter 22

TJ laid her cell phone down after checking one last time for responses from everyone concerning tonight's chat session and picked up her notepad. She checked off everything she needed to do on her end in preparation for the session. According to the responses she'd received, everyone sent a positive reply that they would be there except Dylan. "Who needs her?" TJ said to herself and then put her notepad down, pulled a stick of gum from her backpack, and stuck it in her mouth. She then headed for the Berman home where they all were to meet.

It was a particularly warm Monday evening, and since school was out, everyone basically lay around doing nothing until it was time to head to the Berman home for what TJ and Noi named their Departing Chat Session, which they hoped everyone would attend, but there was still no response from Dylan.

Jermaine was the first to arrive and he walked in and headed straight for Bray's room. He'd made up his mind that he would get there before everyone else just to make sure Bray was up for the session and would be comfortable talking about the accident should he be questioned about it. When he walked into Bray's room, he noticed him sitting with his head down. "Bray, what's up, man? Are you feeling all right?" Bray looked up at him sadly.

"I can't do it, J."

"Can't do what?"

"I can't say goodbye to Dylan tonight. This is our last chat session before she leaves for medical school. Who knows when I will see her again."

"You don't have to worry about seeing Dylan tonight, Bray. I talked to Noi earlier, and she told me Dylan wouldn't be here tonight. She never responded to TJ's text."

"I wish I could say that makes me feel better, but it doesn't." Jermaine walked over and sat down on Bray's bed, turned, and looked out the window and then back at Bray.

"What is it, Bray? What's going on? Did Dylan break up with you?"

"Nope."

"Then what's up? What's going on, Bray?"

"I broke up with her. I also told her I was seeing some-one else." Jermaine started laughing. "What's so funny, J?"

"You, man!" Jermaine laughed more and even harder.

"Hey, fill me in, J, because I fail to see the humor in this." Jermaine tried to stop laughing and catch his breath.

"Please don't tell me Dylan bought that lie, man, please don't!"

"I feel really bad about lying to her, Jermaine, but I didn't know what else to do."

"Tell me, please, Bray, what were you trying to do?"

"I was trying to save her a lot of heartache and disap-pointment later. I don't want Dylan to go on thinking that she and I are going to someday get married. I mean, look at me, J."

"Okay, I'm looking, and what's your point?"

"I'm paralyzed from the waist down, Jermaine. Don't you understand what I'm trying to say here?"

Jermaine walked over to Bray's dresser and picked up a picture of Dylan and Bray at an amusement park one summer. They were hugging and smiling in a selfie picture they'd taken together. Jermaine handed Bray the picture. Bray looked up at him. "I don't understand, Jermaine, why did you hand this to me?"

"How do you feel about the girl in that picture, Bray?"

"Come on, Jermaine, it's Dylan! I can't stop thinking about her, I love her."

"Exactly! Parts of your body are paralyzed, Bray, but not your mind and heart… What I'm trying to say is this, you still think about Dylan and you still have deep affection for her. You love her, Bray. That's all you need, man. The rest will take care of itself. Don't worry about how you will make love to her physically or any other kind of way. When you love someone, Bray, man, you *find* a way to get around the obstacle course. Whatever it is! It's time you stop letting that wheelchair define who you are, Bray. That chair is just a means of you moving around! It's not who you are! There are people in wheelchairs accomplishing the unimaginable in their situation, setting world records, man, living their life to the fullest because they don't focus on being in a wheelchair, Bray, they focus on living, man! Live your life, Bray! Dylan is a very important part of your life, don't push her out of it. If you do, you will regret it.

Here is something else you need to consider when it comes to Dylan. The fact that she is willing to hang in there with you, Bray, still willing to marry you one day, even though you're in a wheelchair, should tell you something. It should tell you how much she loves and cares for you, Bray. So why are you hurting her, pushing her away when she is willing to stay?"

Bray let out a heavy sigh. "Man, J, when did you become so wise?"

"It doesn't take wisdom to see when someone truly cares for another person, Bray, just common sense. Talk to Dylan, fix this mess you've made before she goes off to medical school and returns home on the arm of someone else." Jermaine started laughing again. "Man, I can't believe you lied to her like that, Bray, and she bought it! You mentioned being wise a bit ago. Well, here are some words of wisdom for you…stop lying. You feeling okay about this chat session? I mean, you know they might ask you about the accident, you up for that?"

"Not really, but I will handle it. I'm looking forward to us all being together again since the accident."

"Cool, let's go then!" Jermaine wheeled Bray to the Berman family room where the chat session was to be held.

Noel took her place at the center of the room and called the chat session to order. Sure enough, everyone was there except Dylan. Noel went over the rules and then looked around the room to see if everyone was paying attention. She glanced at Bray and noticed him looking in the direction of the front door. She walked over to him and whispered, "Bray, you okay? Dylan will be here. I know she will. At first, I had my doubts but I think she will show."

"Yeah, I'm fine, Noi." Noel looked at him, then slowly walked back to take her place at the center of the room.

"Okay, let me just reiterate what I just said for clarity." While Noel was going over the rules again, Dylan walked in the room, and they all turned and looked at her. TJ shot a glance at Bray, who had his eyes glued to Dylan.

"Hello, everybody, I'm sorry I'm late. I stopped to pick up Bray's favorite cupcakes. There are enough to share if any of the rest of you would like one." Jermaine looked at Bray, but Bray didn't notice; he was still looking at Dylan.

Noel cleared her throat loudly and said, "This is a special chat session, our parting chat session, and that's because Dylan will be leaving for medical school in a week. Jermaine will be starting college, although driving back and forth every day, and Bray is taking online writing classes. They won't have time for us, so we need to enjoy them while they are still around." Everyone smiled and nodded in agreement to what Noel said.

Bray raised his hand to say something. "Yes, Bray, you have the floor."

"Well, first, the online writing classes are just temporary. I will be starting college next year. Not sure which one yet, but it will be somewhere close to home." He looked over at Dylan and said, "I'm looking forward to a happy and bright future." Dylan gave way to a slow smile, and they all clapped for Bray.

"Anyone else?" Noel said. Dylan raised her hand, and Noel called on her.

"Well, as you all know, I will be starting medical school this fall and I, too, am looking forward to a happy and bright future…with Bray." The room grew still, and then Jermaine started clapping slowly, and soon everyone joined in a thunderous applause for Bray and Dylan.

After a few more comments, Noel thanked them all for coming, called the session to a close, and invited everyone to have a slice of the graduation cake TJ made for Dylan, Bray, and Jermaine. Dylan walked over to the cake and cut herself a slice and then she cut a large slice for Bray and took it to him. Bray looked at her and took the cake. "Dylan, we have to talk. I lied to you and I'm so sorry. I'm not seeing anyone else. I only…"

"Bray, eat your cake," Dylan said. But Bray kept trying to talk, so Dylan gently laid a finger on Bray's lips to silence him. "We will talk later, Bray, but for now, let's just enjoy our cake."

"Okay, but just one more thing Dylan…what made you say what you just did. What makes you so sure we will end up together?"

"In my heart I know we belong together Bray. I feel it and I will not accept anything less." Bray looked at her and smiled, then ate his cake.

*****

Cree glanced up at the antique clock on the fireplace mantle in her living room and she then exhaled slowly and drank from her bottled water. "Hey, Mom," Dylan said as she walked in the house.

"Hey, honey, where were you? I was about to call you. Dylan, it's late."

"I know, I'm sorry, I should have called. I was at the chat…I mean, I was at the Berman's."

"This late? Dylan, it's almost twelve-thirty!"

"I'm sorry, but Bray and I had some things to talk about. That's why I'm so late."

"How is Bray?"

"He is great! He has decided to go to college next year. I'm so excited for him!"

"Dylan, I need to talk to you about something."

"Mom, like you said, it's late and I'm tired. Can this wait until morning, please?"

"It's late because you chose to stay out late, Dylan. Now I understand that you're tired, and trust me, after a day of surgeries and mishaps, I certainly know what that feels like. But we need to address this right now, honey."

"Address? When you say we need to address something, Mom, I know what you mean by that. It means you get to talk and I get to say nothing."

"That's not true, Dylan, and you know it. Look, let's just get this out and discuss it. The sooner we do, the sooner we both get to go to bed." Dylan tossed her purse and jacket in a chair and reluctantly sat down in the one beside it.

"Bray, what's going on with you two?"

"What do you mean?"

"Dylan, I'm not trying to pry. I am just concerned about you, about both of you." Dylan looked at Cree.

"Are you going to finish your bottled water?" Cree looked down at her half-empty bottle of water and then handed it to Dylan.

"Sweetie, I can get you a fresh bottle of water from the fridge. You don't have to drink that."

"It's okay, Mom, I just need a little."

"Are you feeling all right? If the nausea is coming back…"

"No, I'm fine, really."

"Dylan, your bouts with nausea, I think it might be stress related."

"Mom, I'm going on eighteen years old. I don't have that much stress in my life right now."

"Yes, you do. Bray is stress, starting college this fall is stress, just being alive is stressful, although it's certainly better than the alternative."

"Bray and I are fine now, Mom. He told me the truth, he is not seeing anyone. He said he only told me that to push me away from him because of the…because of the accident and he being partially paralyzed now. But we are fine now. We had a long talk tonight and we've decided to get back together and go forward with our original plans to get married after we finish college."

Cree got up and walked to the middle of the floor. "Dylan, you and Bray are still so young yet. You're barely out of high school and you're considering getting married?"

"Not considering, *are* getting married. We are getting married, Mom. I love Bray and he loves me."

"Love? Dylan, again you and Bray are so young still. Do you even know what love is, what it means?"

"I know exactly what it means, and I'm sorry, but I didn't realize that one of the requirements for falling in love with someone, was that you had to be a certain age to do so."

"Dylan, I don't mean to make this difficult for you, but…"

"But you are, Mom, you are making this very difficult. First, because you are my mother and I love you. The last thing I want to do is defy you, but once I turn eighteen, if you try to stand in the way of me marrying Bray, I will. Secondly, I want and need your support. It's just us, Mom, you and me. You are my family, I am your family…we have no one else." Dylan paused. "I need to know I have my family's backing. I need to know I have your support Mom the day Bray and I get married!" Dylan paused again, then softly said, "Mom, this is not about me marrying Bray. This is about me marrying a paraplegic. You think I can't handle it! Well, I can. I'm a lot stronger physically, mentally, and emotionally than you realize!"

"Dylan, taking care of a paraplegic is a lot more involved than you realize I'm afraid. It's going to take money, time, energy, and the patience of Job! Are you sure you're up for that?"

"Mom, that day you came in from work and found me lying on the bathroom floor, you were tired, you had worked all day, probably not even with the benefit of getting to eat lunch. But you found the energy to mix a drink that would help stop my nausea, run a warm bath for me, clean my room, strip my bed, then go to your room and get me an extra pillow so I would be comfortable. All that after a full day of surgeries and consulting with patients, you found the energy and strength to do all that. Do you know why?"

Cree just stared at Dylan and said nothing. "I'll tell you why…because you love me. That's why you were able to take care of me that day, even though you were exhausted. Well, I love Bray, that's why I know I will be able to take care of him. Will it be hard sometimes? Yes, it will, but life is hard at times, yet somehow we get through it. I love you, Mom. I'm tired, please, may I be excused now?" Cree slowly nodded her head yes and said, "Good night." "Good night, mom." Cree just stared at Dylan as she walked off to bed, then said to herself, "Sleep well Dylan."

Chapter 23

"Okay, son," Waverly said as she pointed to the button on Bray's smartwatch. "If you need anything, all you have to do is dial Pam's number that is programmed into your smartwatch and Pam will come running! Right, Pam?" Waverly turned and said to Pam as she stood watching Waverly go over instructions with Bray. Today was the first day of Waverly's return to work. She was nervous, not about returning to work but about leaving Bray to someone else's care and keeping. "Pam, you have my cell number, pager number, and the number to the hospital if you need me, right?"

Pam smiled and said, "Yes ma'am, I've got all of your numbers, Dr. Berman. Bray and I are going to be just fine, don't you worry."

Bray looked up at his mom and gave her a smile of reassurance. "Pam is right, Mom. We are going to be fine. Don't you worry. Dylan will be here at two and Jermaine at five. Of course, Noi and Ellis are always here unfortunately."

"Bray?"

"Sorry, Mom, just kidding. Seriously, we are going to be fine. Have a good first day back to work."

MY FATHER, MY SON

Waverly looked at Pam. "Take good care of him Pam, please."

"I will, you have my promise." Waverly walked over and bent down in front of Bray's wheelchair.

"If you need anything, even if it's just to talk to me, you call me. Don't worry about interrupting anything at work. You call me Bray, do you hear me?"

"Mom?"

"Bray, do you hear me?"

"Yes, ma'am."

"Good. I love you, son." Bray reached up and put his arms around his mother.

"I love you, too, Mom. Have a good day."

*****

"Well, good morning, welcome back," Cree said to Waverly as she walked into the hospital cafeteria. "Come on, I'll buy you a coffee and a plate of eggs. How is that for a first-day welcome back?" Waverly laughed.

"You're the best!"

"Dr. Berman, how are you doing? Good to see you and welcome back. I was so sorry to hear about your son's accident. So sorry," Matt, the cafeteria manager, said as Cree and Waverly walked to the register to pay for their breakfast. After paying for their breakfast, they found a small table in the corner of the room.

"So how is it going? You okay?"

"Yeah, I guess. I don't have the warm fuzzies about returning to work. I still worry about Bray, even though

I'm confident that Pam is very capable of taking good care of him."

"Of course you do, you're his mother. But try to relax, it's going to be okay, Waverly."

"Is it?" Cree looked at Waverly, and before she could respond, she was paged over the hospital intercom.

"Paging Dr. Hayes, paging Dr. Cree Hayes! You are needed in emergency, *stat*!"

"Welcome back, let's go!" Waverly and Cree jumped up from the table and ran out of the cafeteria, leaving their coffee and eggs untouched.

When they reached the emergency room, they noticed a young girl breathing heavily; her mom was hysterical! "What's up?" Cree shouted to the nurse working on the child.

"Fifteen-year-old, accidentally struck in the head by a teammate during a soccer game at school!"

"My baby, oh my god, my baby!" the mother cried out.

"Miss, Miss, please! You will have to wait outside!" Cree said to the mother.

"No, I will not wait outside!"

"My god, the blood is pouring from this child's head like a broken fire hydrant! We have to get her to surgery right away, see what's going on with this gash and inside her head!"

"Yes, Doctor!"

"No, my child!" Cree looked at the mother.

"Ma'am, we are going to do all we can to help your daughter, okay? But for now, please wait outside! Nurse, have operating room 5 set up immediately and arrange for nurse assistance." She then turned to Waverly and said,

"Let's go!" Waverly hesitated. "Waverly, what's wrong with you? Let's go. I need assistance with this surgery right now! Are you up for this?" Waverly nodded her head yes. "Okay, so let's go! Now! Right now!"

Twenty-five minutes later, Waverly found herself sitting outside of operating room 5 and trying to figure out what went wrong. "Why did I lose my focus, my concentration, while working on that fifteen-year-old?" she asked herself. Her mind had become a mass of confusion, and Cree had to take over. Three hours later, after walking out of Simon Memorial Hospital, Waverly found herself sitting at her kitchen table. She couldn't believe she'd quit her job, just walked out of the hospital after Cree had tried to tell her to get some help.

"Mom? What are you doing here! Why are you not still at work?" Bray asked as he wheeled himself into the kitchen closer to his mother.

"Hey, son, how are you feeling? Everything going okay with Pam?"

"Yeah, sure! Mom, what's going on? Have you been crying?"

"I'm okay, Bray, I'm fine," Waverly said as her voice broke and she started to cry. She then quickly wiped her eyes and straightened up in her chair. Bray took her hand in his.

"Mom, what is it? Talk to me."

"I just quit my job, Bray. Isn't that ridiculous?" Waverly said as her voice began to break again. Bray looked at her.

"You quit your job? Why, what happened?"

"I don't know. I honestly don't know. This fifteen-year-old girl was rushed into the hospital from a blow to the head. She was bleeding profusely and needed surgery. In the middle of operating on her, I lost it… Everything just went blank, and I couldn't…I couldn't remember what to do next, so Cree had to take over."

"Mom, it's okay, it's all right. Please don't worry. You are going to be okay, no, you are okay. You are an excellent doctor. You will find another job."

As if she hadn't heard a word Bray just said, Waverly looked at him through tear-filled eyes and said, "Cree thinks I need help, professional help. I'm beginning to think she is right."

"Mom, you don't need professional help, you just need rest."

Noel walked in from her summer job at the grocery store and looked at her mother and then at Bray quizzically. "Mom just quit her job, Noi."

"What! Mom, why? Are you okay?"

"She is fine, Noi."

"No, she is not fine! She is sitting right in front of us Bray, and forgive me but you are partially paralyzed, not blind! Clearly she is not fine! Mom, what's wrong? Just tell me who I need to punch!" They all laughed, and Waverly started to feel better.

"Mom, go to your room and lie down. Noi and I will take care of dinner, right, Noi?"

"Sure, of course. Where are we ordering from, Bray?"

"I don't know, but there are about a hundred menu choices in that drawer over there. I'm sure we can come up with something." Waverly smiled and picked a napkin out of the napkin holder on the table and dried her eyes. She then sighed and went up to her room to take a nap.

*****

"You are not quitting on me, I won't allow it. It's not an option, Waverly." Waverly was sitting out on the deck with a glass of wine in her hands, looking out over the lake when she turned to see Cree standing behind her. She'd come down from her nap an hour earlier and eaten the dinner Noi and Bray ordered from an Indian restaurant and delivered by Uber Eats.

"Mom, are you okay?" Cree and Waverly turned to see Ellis standing in the doorway behind them and looking at Waverly anxiously.

"Hey, Ellis, yes, son, I'm fine."

"Hello, Ellis."

"Hi, Dr. Hayes. I was just checking on Mom."

"Sure, son, of course."

"Well, I will see you later, Mom. I'm going skating with some of the guys from school, I won't be long. Good night, Dr. Hayes."

"Good night, Ellis." After Ellis left, Cree looked at Waverly, who had turned back to staring at the lake. "Waverly, may I sit down? Please?"

"Sure, Cree, I'm not upset with you. I'm upset with myself for falling apart in the operating room today. I've been a doctor, a surgeon, for years. That was not supposed to happen."

"Being a doctor doesn't make you infallible. You have the same right as everyone else to get confused, tired, to make a mistake, and hurt. All of those things collided in that operating room today, causing you to lose your focus, your concentration. I want you to take another month, do what you must, whatever it is, to get yourself together. Concentrate on you, Waverly, mentally and physically. Bray is doing great. He is a warrior and he will survive and come out of this carrying a torch of victory. You have a nurse to help care for him now. Let her do her job and you take care of yourself." Waverly looked at Cree.

"Cree, I'm afraid I've forgotten how to do that."

"It's okay, I'm here. I'll help you remember how to." Cree got up and walked over to Waverly, bent down, and hugged her.

"What's going on out here!"

"Ms. Purlasky, Megan! What a pleasant surprise! Come sit down and join us!"

"Don't mind if I do," Ms. Purlasky said while Megan lingered in the background, standing in the doorway. Ms. Purlasky turned around and looked at her daughter. "Megan! Come, come quickly! Why are you standing there like that, child?"

"Kerry is on his way over to our place. We can't stay too long, you know that!"

"Kerry this, Kerry that! Kerry, Kerry, Kerry. I tell you, my daughter has Kerry Stupidity! You go Megan. Cree will bring me home, won't you, Cree?" Cree looked at Ms. Purlasky with her mouth hung open. "Close your mouth, Cree, before something flies in it," Ms. Purlasky said as she pulled up another chair on the deck, pulled off her shoes, and then propped her feet up in it. Cree and Waverly just looked at her and then shook their head.

"Sure, of course, I will take you home. You get home, Megan, don't want to keep hubby to be waiting."

"Thank you, Dr. Hayes."

Megan rushed off, leaving the three of them to talk. "Where is our beautiful boy, our Bray, this evening? How is he doing?"

"Ms. Purlasky, Bray is doing just fine, looking forward to taking online classes this fall and starting regular college next fall."

"Wonderful, that's wonderful news."

"Any word from the police concerning his accident? Have they caught the person yet?"

Waverly set her glass of wine down and looked out into the distance before saying, "I'm afraid not, Ms. Purlasky. Strange, I don't know why, but I get the feeling Bray knows who hit him on Lombar Road that night. But for some reason, he won't say. He just keeps saying the same thing over and over whenever anyone asks him about that night. He just says 'I've told you all I can' and then shuts down."

"Waverly, let me tell you something. Your mind is telling you that Bray knows who hit him for a reason. Don't ignore it. Sometimes we ignore the obvious simply because we don't want to face reality." Cree looked at Ms. Purlasky because she knew all too well that she was telling the truth. She, too, had a nagging feeling that Bray knows who caused his accident but just will not say. Why, is what she couldn't figure out.

"Ms. Purlasky, I'm sorry but I've got an early surgery scheduled tomorrow. Would you mind me taking you home now?"

"No, not at all. Waverly, give me a to-go cup of that wine so Cree and I can be on our way."

Waverly smiled and said, "Yes, ma'am!"

After Cree and Ms. Purlasky left, Waverly poured herself another glass of wine and then used the chair that Ms. Purlasky had put her feet up on to prop her own feet up. She looked up at a beautiful sunset and started to relax.

Chapter 24

Jermaine parked his truck on Lombar Road and then got out of it and stretched his back. It was dusk and he knew he should be heading home but the license plate he'd seen there earlier would not leave him alone. He had to find it, he felt. He locked the door of his jeep and walked in the direction he saw it last, as always keeping his eyes glued to the ground. He walked up and down Lombar Road for hours it seemed before he spotted it. It was somewhat hidden under a bush. He rushed to it but stopped before picking it up. "Man, that thing is filthy, and what are those red spots all over it? I hope it's not blood."

Jermaine ran back to his truck, pulled out a pair of work gloves, and thanked his summer job as a gardener for making the gloves available to him. He put the gloves on and then ran back to the spot where he saw the license plate and picked it up. When he got back to his truck, he said to himself, "I'm going to show this to Dad as soon as I get home. Maybe it will mean something, help us find who caused Bray's accident."

When Jermaine pulled up in his parking spot at home, Noel was sitting on the porch waiting for him. He got out and walked up to her. "Hey, Noi! What's up? What brings you here? Is Bray okay?"

"Yeah, he is fine. I just stopped by to bring you these." Jermaine laughed.

"What are these?"

"Here, silly, take the bag and look in it." Jermaine took the bag from Noel and looked in it. "They are pistachios and you love them. I was at the mall and I thought to myself 'Jermaine is so good to Bray and the rest of my family I ought to buy him something.' I remember hearing you tell Bray one time how much you loved them, so I bought you some."

Jermaine reached out and hugged Noel. "Thank you, Noi, but you didn't have to do this. I love you and your family. I'm here for you guys now and always. Like I said, you didn't have to do this, but I appreciate you thinking about me and I will definitely enjoy them because you were thoughtful enough to buy them for me."

"Well, I've got to get home, J. See you tomorrow…I mean, you are coming over to see Bray, right?"

"You know I'll be there!"

"Great, see you then."

After Noel walked off heading home, Jermaine called to her, "Hey, Noi, do you want me to take you home?"

"No thanks, I'm okay. It's only a twenty-minute walk from here, and I could use the exercise. Night, J."

"Night, Noi." Jermaine continued to watch Noel walk off. "Man, what a looker. Too bad she is only fifteen and Bray's little sister. Oh well." Jermaine walked in the house, forgetting he had the license plate in the car on the floor, and ran up to shower.

After Jermaine stepped out of the shower and dried off, he walked to his bedroom to check his cell phone for any messages from Bray. An entire day had lapsed without either of them texting or calling, which was unusual. He threw on a pair of sweats and a T-shirt, fell across his bed, and sent Bray a text. "Hey, man, what's up? How you doing?"

Bray replied right back, "Hey, J! I'm good, man! Where you been all day? I was about to call you!"

"I had to work today. You know, I'm holding down a summer job to help dad with college expenses."

There was a twelve-minute pause before Bray responded, "I understand. Nice that you got that scholarship. I'm sure that is helping!"

"Definitely, but it's not a full scholarship, so we still have a little to pay. With Dad's savings for my schooling and my working this summer, by the time I start college, it will be paid for."

"Nice!"

"Noi was just here, brought me over some pistachios!"

"LOL, I think my little sister has a crush on you, J." Jermaine looked at Bray's response and thought about it for a few minutes before replying.

"You might be right, Bray, but Noi is only fifteen, I'm seventeen."

"Two-year difference, J, come on, man!"

"Yeah, I know, Bray, but she is still only fifteen and she is your little sister. I'm not feeling it. Maybe in a few years. Maybe?"

"I hear you! Well, I got to go. Dylan leaves for medical school tomorrow, so Mom is taking me to her house. We are going to dress up in the outfits we bought for the prom but didn't get to wear because of my car accident and wear them to dinner tonight."

"Awesome! Enjoy dinner, Bray. Talk to you later!"

*****

Dylan stuffed her last suitcase as much as she could with clothes, jewelry, and anything else she could make fit in it. She then tried to zip it up only to have the zipper break because there were just too many things in that one bag. Cree walked in just as Dylan let out an "Oh no!"

"Really, Dylan, what made you think you could fit a full-size closet worth of things into an overnight size bag?"

"Mom, I'm tired! I just want to get the last of this stuff packed and relax a little. Plus, Dr. Berman is bringing Bray by to see me off in a few minutes, and I want no distractions!"

Cree smiled. "How was dinner last night and where did you guys go?"

"Dinner was amazing, and we went to Raphael's. Gorgeous! The food is out of this world!"

"Raphael's? That's one of Jessica's dad's French restaurants over on Emerson Street. How in the world were you or Bray able to pay for dinner there? The appetizers alone start at one-hundred-dollars!"

"Aunt Jess paid for us. She took care of everything, even gave Bray and me our own private room. When I told her how Bray and I planned to spend our night before me going off to college, she said to me 'Just leave everything to me.' Mom, everything was so nice!"

"I'm happy for you, honey, and Bray. So glad you had a good time. Girl, that black dress you wore last night was nothing short of breathtaking!"

"Thank you, Mom. It sure cost enough. I almost put it back you know."

"Oh, I know how much it cost, I got the bill!" They both laughed. "Take all that stuff out of that suitcase, sweetie. I'm going to my room to get you a bigger one to transfer your things to."

Just as Cree and Dylan finished transferring things from the smaller suitcase to the larger one Cree found in her room, Cree's cell phone rang. She looked down at the number. "It's Aunt Jess," she said to Dylan before answering.

"Hey, Jess!"

"Hey, come open your front door before all this stuff falls out of my hands and arms!"

"Girl, what have you done? What have you bought Dylan now?"

"Come!"

"Okay, on my way!" As soon as Cree opened the door, Jessica staggered in with bags and bags of newly bought sheets, towels, toiletries, and other items for Dylan to take off to college with her. Cree took a few bags from her arms, and Jessica struggled to the sofa and let the rest of the bags fall onto it. She then flopped down on the little bit of space left on the sofa beside the bags.

"Hey, Aunt Jess! Oh my gosh, you bought me designer bedding! Thanks, Aunt Jess," Dylan said as she ran over and threw her arms around Jessica. Cree stood holding the designer bedclothes and linens in her hands while looking at Jessica as if she'd lost her mind.

"Jess, I can't believe you spent all this money on bedding for Dylan! She is going off to college, not buying her first house!"

"For heaven's sakes, Cree, calm down and live a little! Reap the benefits of Dad's success, I sure do!" Cree just shook her head.

"Moderation, Jess, everything in moderation. That's what I'm trying to instill in Dylan."

"Well, good for you, and besides, I bought a modest number of things for Dylan. God knows I wanted to buy more, but I was too tired to lift another thing into my basket." Dylan laughed and noticed Jessica's hair.

"Aunt Jess, I love your hair! When did you go blond? I thought it was red last night."

"It was. I changed it to blond today. You like?"

"Yep, I think it's cool! What do you think, Mom?" Cree looked at Jessica's hair.

"I think it's pretty and, Jess, you'd better be glad you have all that hair because when it starts to break from color treating it so much, at least you will still have a lot left on your head!"

"Whatever, Cree!"

"Dylan, come here, sweetie," Jessica said as she got up and walked to the window. "Come look out the window and tell Aunt Jess what you see." Dylan ran to the window and peeped out of the plantation shutters and then let out such a loud scream it scared Cree.

"What? What is it, Dylan?" Dylan didn't hear a word Cree said; she turned to Jessica and said, "Is it mine? Is it, Aunt Jess?"

"It most certainly is, a 2019, and paid for!"

Cree walked swiftly to the shutters and peeped out herself and then whirled around to stare at Jessica. "Now, Cree, calm down, just calm yourself! It's not that bad! It's just a little old jeep, that's all it is! Just breathe, you will be fine, you will get used to it!"

"Jessica, that is a Jeep Grand Cherokee! Take it back, take it right back right now! Dylan has a car, and it's working just fine!"

"Mom!"

"Take it back, Jess, I mean it!"

Jessica put her hands on her hips and looked at Cree. "Dylan's car is about to fall apart and you know it! It has about, what, six miles left on it? She needs a reliable car while away at school, Cree! Do you want her to trust Ms. Dilapidated to get her from point A to point B? I mean, heaven forbid, she's out one night while away at school and that thing just cuts off on her! Is that what you want?"

Cree just looked at Jessica. She didn't want to admit it, but she did have a good point.

"Please, Cree, let her keep it."

"Yeah, Mom! Please let me keep it! I love it, and it's white, my favorite color!" Cree shot Dylan a warning glance.

"Cree, ever since Dylan was born, you've worked yourself into the ground trying to provide for her, never asking anyone for help because of that foolish pride of yours. You have done an amazing job raising Dylan. Look at her," Jessica said while pointing to Dylan. "She's beautiful inside and out, she's smart, and she's going to college on a scholarship she earned because you instilled in her the importance to excel in whatever she did and to treat others with kind-

271

ness and respect. I witnessed her upbringing, Cree, so I can say these things from firsthand knowledge. It's time you let someone help you, Cree. You know, if it were not for you, I would never have had that mastectomy, and heaven only knows what state my health would be in right now. Today, thanks to you, I'm cancer free and enjoying my life. I owe you!"

"Jessica, you don't owe me anything."

"Okay, well, this is my graduation gift to Dylan. It's a gift, Cree, to Dylan from me. Please don't deny me this. Even though our friendship ended back home, I'm still her godmother, a privilege you gave me before you dumped me."

"I didn't dump you."

"Yes, you did. Anyway, can she keep the car, please?" Cree looked from Jessica to Dylan and then back to Jessica.

"Well, she does need reliable transportation, and I certainly don't want my child stuck on the side of the road somewhere because her car broke down on her or for any other reason." Cree gave way to a half smile. "Okay, she can keep it. I appreciate you doing this for Dylan, Jess, and I love you." Dylan and Jessica both let out a scream and then ran over and bearhugged Cree.

Waverly and Bray arrived at Dylan's house a little later than expected due to complications with getting his wheelchair settled in the back of Waverly's new car, which was considerably smaller than her old one, the one totaled as a result of the accident. Dylan was a little nervous, thinking they would not make it before she, Jessica, and her mom left for VCU School of Medicine.

"I can't believe this is finally it. You are getting ready to leave for school right now, today!"

"I'm leaving for school, Bray, not leaving you. Just remember that."

"I know. Still, it's hard, Dylan."

"Every day, just like we discussed after the last Monday Night Chat Session, we call and text every single day, Bray. No matter what happens during our day, we reach out to each other every day."

"That's not going to be a problem, Dylan. My day wouldn't be right without you in it, whether you are here with me or on the phone."

Dylan looked at Bray and then leaned over and hugged him so tightly he could hardly breathe. Ignoring his discomfort, he hugged her back just as tightly.

"Okay, guys, I hate to break this up, but it's getting late, and we really need to hit the road. Dylan, Aunt Jess and I have packed everything in your new car, and she is going to follow us in it." Dylan pulled away from Bray reluctantly and fought back tears. Bray looked at her and smiled.

"The holidays will be here soon, Dylan, and we will be together again."

"Mom, just one more second alone with Bray, please?"

Cree smiled and walked away. Dylan then turned to Bray and said, "I love you, Bray. Call you when we get to VCU."

"I love you, too, Dylan."

Chapter 25

Eight years later

Cree and Waverly sat at Waverly's kitchen table and nursed their cups of coffee as they reflected on years gone by. Neither of them could believe their children were all grown-up now. Bray completed his online writing courses and was now in his last year of college. To his credit, he'd already written and published three best-selling books. Jermaine graduated law school with honors and was working as a patent attorney for the Taverston law firm of Wilson and James. To everyone's surprise, Jermaine and Noel were dating now that she was older.

Waverly looked at Cree and smiled. "How does it feel to have Dylan home now and starting work at Simon Memorial tomorrow?"

"It feels great! I can't believe eight years have passed since Jessica and I took her to VCU for her first day of medical school!"

"Time goes by quickly. Oh, you guys are coming to the ceremony being held for Bray at Raymond DeMassi, right?"

"Wouldn't miss it for the world."

Cree's cell phone rang, and she picked up the call from Ms. Purlasky whose happiness could be heard for miles.

"It's a girl, it's a girl! My Megan just gave birth to a beautiful baby girl, and she looks just like her grandmother, well, of course she does. I'm beautiful!"

Cree laughed and said to Waverly, "It's Ms. Purlasky. Megan had the baby, and it's a girl."

"Cree, I have to run now. Kerry is calling me. He wants me to come and hold my new granddaughter. Oh, I can't believe it! It seems like only yesterday he and Megan were married!"

"You go to your family, Ms. Purlasky. Congratulations and can't wait to meet your new granddaughter. What is her name?"

"Her name is Star, Star Berlin Monroe. Berlin is my middle name, oh, I'm so proud! I've got to go, talk to you soon!"

Jessica walked in the kitchen and poured herself a cup of coffee. "Nevin let me in. Sorry I'm late, but the restaurant was crazy tonight. I think everyone but you guys were there tonight. There were so many people, faces I haven't seen before."

"Waverly, Jessica has some great news!" Jessica quickly set her cup of coffee down and smiled.

"Yes, I do! I got my test results back today, and there is still absolutely no trace of cancer in my body. It's been eight years, and thanks to Cree, I'm still here and doing well. Oh, and guess what!"

"What?" Cree and Waverly said in unison.

"I have a date with that cute Dr. Avery. I met him when I visited you at the hospital last, Cree!"

"What! No way!" Waverly said.

"Way!" Jessica said.

"I am so happy for you, Jess," Cree said as she looked at Jessica and smiled.

*****

Robbie McBride stared at the license plate Jermaine had brought in to him. Jermaine discovered the license plate while pulling a pair of shoes from under the back seat of his jeep. He had been so involved with law school and studying he had forgotten it was there.

Robbie reluctantly picked up the phone and called the Berman home. Waverly answered, "Waverly, it's Robbie. I need to come by. Is Nevin home because I need to speak to both of you, together."

"Robbie, what's wrong?" Robbie didn't respond to Waverly's question; he just told her he would be there soon. When he arrived, Nevin and Waverly invited him in and walked him into Nevin's office so they could speak privately. Waverly sensed that whatever Robbie had to say to them had to be said without their children hearing.

Robbie looked at Nevin sadly. "Nevin, we ran a check on a license plate Jermaine gave me this morning. He'd had it in the back of his truck for years and forgot it was there. We ran the check because the paint colors and chips found on the license plate matched the color of the car Bray was driving the night of his accident." Robbie looked down at the floor and then back up at Nevin and Waverly.

"Nevin, it took some time and a lot of searching because eight years have passed, but we were able to find who the license plate belonged to."

"Oh, thank God, we are going to finally learn who put my boy in that wheelchair," Nevin said with tears in his eyes.

Robbie stared at Nevin, his heart breaking for him, Waverly, their family. "Nevin, *the person is you.* The license plate was registered to you." Robbie let out a nervous sigh. "I can't arrest you because of the statute of limitations for such a crime here in Taverston, which is four years. But I just thought you should know."

Waverly looked at Nevin, who looked like he was about to pass out. "I'm very sorry. I will leave you two to discuss this among yourselves and with your family." With that, Robbie walked out of the house. Silence, usually so comforting, threatened to suffocate Waverly and she almost wished it would. Nevin looked so pale Waverly feared he would expire right on the spot. Nevin lost touch with reality for a few minutes while thinking he was somehow still awake yet part of a tragic nightmare.

Finally he said, "All this time I was thinking it was a deer I hit that night on Lombar Road, a deer," Nevin said as his voice started to break. "I hit my son, Bray, oh dear God. Waverly, I hit our son, Bray. I'm sorry, I'm so sorry. I paralyzed our boy. He begged me to get some help before it was too late." Nevin got up and tried to walk out of the room. He was devastated and didn't know where to go or what to do. All he knew was that he had to get out of the house. He looked at Waverly and then sat back down and cried.

Waverly looked at Nevin. "I knew, somehow in the back of my mind, I knew, but I couldn't bring myself to accept it."

"Waverly, I am so sorry. I am going to pack my things and leave," Nevin said while wiping away his tears.

"No, you are not going anywhere, Nevin. This is the part where I should scream and yell at you, hit and punch you, but what good would it do? Am I heartbroken, devastated? Yes, I am. My heart is pounding so hard I fear I might have a heart attack, but I must hold myself together for my children, and you must hold yourself together for your family as our head."

After Nevin and Waverly called their children together and explained to Ellis, Noi, and Bray that a license plate had been found, registered to their father, with paint colors and chips on it that matched the color of the car Bray was driving the night of his accident, a calmness came over the house, a calmness in their home that none of them had experienced in a long time.

Surprisingly, Ellis was the first one to speak up. "Dad made a mistake, a tragic mistake, but a mistake, nonetheless. I don't want him to go to jail." Noel walked over and hugged her father before saying, "We love you, Dad."

Bray stared at his father and then looked around the room at his family and smiled. "I guess I should be sad, but I'm not. I'm happy. I'm happy because out of tragedy came triumph. I didn't die that night in that accident, and we have our father back.

I know my father loves me, his son, and he would have never deliberately hit me that night on Lombar Road." Waverly looked at Bray because he had just confirmed her suspicion, that he knew all along that it was his father that hit him head on that night on Lombar Road.

Nevin walked over to Bray and put his arms around him, repeating over and over what he'd been saying to him ever since he learned that he was the one who hit Bray and caused him to be partially paralyzed, "I'm sorry, I'm so very sorry, son."

Bray looked up at his father and said, "It's okay, Dad. I forgive you."

Waverly looked around at her family. "The fact that your father will have to look at his son every day and know that he caused him to be partially paralyzed is the ultimate punishment for him. No number of years in prison will ever punish him more than this fact."

The news that Nevin was the cause of Bray's accident spread quickly throughout Taverston. Waverly and Nevin had to endure a lot of criticism and ostracism, but they stuck together and forged ahead daily with the help and support of their children, Cree, Dylan, Jermaine, Jessica, Ms. Purlasky, and the Monroes.

Chapter 26

People filed into the large auditorium the night of the ceremony for Bray to acknowledge his scholastic and basketball achievements and, more importantly, to applaud his endurance, courage and success under the most trying circumstances, being a paraplegic at such a young age. Once everyone was seated, the high school principal at Raymond DeMassi thanked everyone for coming and said a few more opening remarks before calling Bray up to face and speak to the audience.

Bray wheeled himself to the center of the stage and looked out at the audience as a few of the attendees mumbled under their breath and shook their heads. He waited for the audience to calm down and be quiet before he spoke.

"As I look out over the audience tonight, I see faces that I've known all my life and I want to thank you from the bottom of my heart for being here in support of me and my family and to acknowledge my accomplishments under severe trial." Bray paused before continuing. "However, I'm going to focus not just on myself in what I am about to say to you but on me and my family. Without them, my adversity would have been next to impossible to overcome.

The family, what makes up a family, what holds a family together. A family is made up of people bound together by flesh and blood, of course. But a family is so much more than that. A family is made up of strength, support, forgiveness when needed the most and unconditional love."

Bray looked at Jermaine, who was sitting in the front of the audience. "A family is also made up of friendship that transcends the definition found in the dictionary and grasps the love expressed by only a true friend, a loyal friend, and a friend who treats you as family. I love you, J.

Taverston is a very small town, and news travels fast. I know you all are aware that my father has been the one found to have caused my accident on Lombar Road several years ago, the accident that resulted in me being in this wheelchair. I also know many of you are asking, how? How is it that I am able to look at my father every day and not hate him for putting me in this wheelchair? Well, the answer is simple. He is the head, the pillar of support for my family. I know that my father would have never deliberately hit me that night on Lombar Road, and I have forgiven him for doing so. I love my father enough to look past that one tragic night on Lombar Road, to the memories my mind and heart will not let me erase.

The memories. The memories of what my father has done and is doing to care for his family. The sacrifices he has made for the benefit of his family. Sacrifices too numerous to share with you tonight. But I will share these memories that I hold dear to my heart. I remember my father holding down two jobs so my mother could attend medical school and not have to work, coming home so tired sometimes he could hardly hold his head up. But before he went to bed, he always asked me, Noi, and Ellis if we'd eaten, although he didn't have the strength to.

The memory of the day I tried at seven years old to learn to ride my bike and kept falling off. Dad would pick me up and put me back on it and then tell me to keep trying until finally I was able to stay up on the bike on my own. The memory of the day he said to me, 'Son, when everyone else turns their back and walks away from you, I'll still be standing in front of you.'"

Bray looked out into the audience at his father, placed his hand over his heart, and said in a loud voice, "My father."

Nevin looked up on the stage at Bray with tears in his eyes, put his hand over his heart, and said in a loud voice, "My son."

Bray then smiled, looked out into the audience, and said, "I'm happy, so I ask all of you to please be happy for me and my family. Good night."

Two years later

Waverly walked over to the table that held the wedding cake for Dylan and Bray and then looked over at the table that held the wedding cake for Noel and Jermaine. Cree walked up and nudged her on the shoulder. "Can you believe this? Our babies just got married today in a double wedding ceremony! I mean, can you stand it!"

Waverly laughed and said, "I had to pinch myself before walking over to have some of this cake. It just doesn't seem real."

The DJ was playing upbeat dance music as Jessica danced her way over to Waverly and Cree then said, "Last one on that dance floor buys dinner for all three of us next weekend!" Cree and Waverly followed Jessica to the dance floor, and soon even more people joined them on the floor and danced to the song "Celebration!"

*****

Waverly and Bray sat at the Berman Family's kitchen table and spoke quietly to each other. "Mom, my accident. Whenever I was asked about it, my answer was the same… I've told you all I can, did I lie?" Waverly reached over and touched Bray's hand.

"Bray, you never said you didn't know who hit you. Had you done so, yes, you would have lied. Again, you never said that, only…I've told you all I can. Your reasoning behind saying this, no one can say. Now eat your blueberry pancakes son, they are getting cold." They both smiled and Bray ate his pancakes.

"IT IS ESTIMATED THAT ABOUT 28 PEOPLE DIE EVERY DAY IN CAR CRASHES."

"CAR ACCIDENTS ARE THE LEADING CAUSE OF SPINAL CORD INJURIES IN THE UNITED STATES."

A MESSAGE FROM LINDA MCCAIN: please think and don't drink if you are about to operate any moving vehicle...it's a matter of life and death.

About the Author

Linda McCain loves to write, as she finds it very therapeutic and feels that a good author should write not for their benefit but the benefit of others. While in college, she majored in Secretarial Science and wrote poetry to escape the world of required study for her classes, and submitted her first article to Essence Magazine on "The Cruelty of Child Abuse." From this, her love for writing grew!

One of Linda's greatest joys in life is serving others by doing Volunteer Work such as raising money for St. Jude's Children's Research Hospital, coordinating a Canned Food Drive for the mentally challenged residents at Washington DC's Woodley House, and helping to coordinate a Clothing Drive for the Homeless.

My Father, My Son is her second book. Linda is currently working on her third book, *Good night Mr. White*, and enjoying the progress of the story but not the essential editing of it.

> *At the end of the day it's not about what you have or even what you've accomplished…it's about who you've lifted up, who you've made better. It's about what you've given back.*
>
> *—Denzel Washington*

CPSIA information can be obtained
at www.ICGtesting.com
Printed in the USA
BVHW071455190720
584039BV00005B/35/J